Francis Morgan Nichols

Mirabilia vrbis Romae. The Marvel of Rome

Or a Picture of the Golden City

Francis Morgan Nichols

Mirabilia vrbis Romae. The Marvel of Rome
Or a Picture of the Golden City

ISBN/EAN: 9783744780162

Printed in Europe, USA, Canada, Australia, Japan

Cover: Foto ©ninafisch / pixelio.de

More available books at **www.hansebooks.com**

THE MARVELS OF ROME

PART OF THE BRONZE DOOR OF SAINT PETER'S.   SEE PAGE 196.

MIRABILIA VRBIS ROMAE

THE
MARVELS OF ROME

OR

A PICTURE OF THE GOLDEN CITY

AN ENGLISH VERSION OF THE MEDIEVAL GUIDE-BOOK
WITH A SUPPLEMENT OF ILLUSTRATIVE MATTER
AND NOTES BY

FRANCIS MORGAN NICHOLS

LONDON. ELLIS AND ELVEY
ROME. SPITHOEVER
1889

PREFACE

THE little book of which an English verſion is here publiſhed for the firſt time was the ſtandard guide-book of the more learned viſitors to Rome from the twelfth to the fifteenth century. Its ſtatements were received with the reſpect due to a work of authority, and their influence may be traced in the writings of many of the authors who flouriſhed during that period. The moſt ſtriking example of the long-ſuſtained credit of the medieval Roman Topography is afforded by the Letters of Petrarch. In the deſcriptions of Rome given by this great leader of the Revival of Learning, ſcarcely any trace appears of the new critical ſpirit, but the localities are ſtill preſented under the names, and aſſociated with the legends, of the *Mirabilia*.

In the following century, when the wider ftudy of ancient authors and infcriptions had impaired its influence among the learned, the *Mirabilia* ftill maintained its place in popular eftimation; and, after the invention of printing, feveral editions of it iffued from the prefs.

In the prefent day this treatife is ufeful to the archæologift as fupplying fome fcanty evidence refpecting the hiftory of the fites and buildings of ancient Rome. Under the perplexing veil of an often arbitrary or barbarous nomenclature it exhibits a fhadowy picture of the ruins which attracted notice in the medieval city, many of which have fince difappeared, while it narrates with charming fimplicity the legends with which the principal monuments, and the few works of art which were not buried beneath the furface, were affociated in the minds of the more educated people of the time.

It fhould be added, in eftimating the

significance of the *Mirabilia*, that the existence and diffusion of the book supply the strongest evidence of the new spirit of curiosity and reverence that had arisen in the twelfth century in regard to the works of ancient art and architecture, which had for many centuries been so ruthlessly destroyed. We should probably not be wrong if we ascribed to this book a powerful influence in the preservation of some at least of the few ruins of importance which still existed in Rome at the time when it was compiled.

Among modern readers, it is not only to the professed archæologist that the *Mirabilia* commends itself. Its delightful legends, and the many natural touches which occur even among the dry lists of Gates, Arches and Ruins, illustrate in the most lively way the manner of thinking which prevailed in the age when it was written, and in the long period during which it continued to be accepted as an authority, when the element of the Marvellous maintained fo important a place in every department of knowledge. It poffeffes the fame charm as a chapter of the Travels of Mandeville, with the advantage that the defcriptions have a more folid foundation of fact, and the objects defcribed are to an ordinary educated perfon more familiar and for the moft part more interefting.

Nothing is known concerning the authorfhip of the book, nor anything of its age or hiftory beyond what may be gathered from the internal evidence of its contents, from the character of the manufcripts in which it has been handed down to us, and from the changes which have at different periods been introduced into its text. For an account of the manufcripts of the *Mirabilia*, the reader may be referred to the critical editions which have been publifhed of the Latin original. It will be fufficient here to give a fummary ftatement of what is known refpecting its text.

The earlieſt extant copy appears to be found in a manuſcript of the Vatican Library (Cod. Vat. 3973), attributed to the end of the twelfth century, and in which it is preceded by a liſt of popes, which ended originally with Celeſtine III., who ruled from 1191 to 1198, and followed by the Chronicle of Romualdus, Archbiſhop of Salerno, ending in the year 1178. Another manuſcript of the ſame library, attributed to the thirteenth century, contains the *Mirabilia* in the ſame volume with the *Digeſta pauperis ſcholaris Albini* (deacon under Pope Lucius III. 1181-1185), and with extracts from the *Politicus* of Benedictus Canonicus (written before 1142), and from the writings of Cencius Camerarius, afterwards Pope Honorius III. (1216-1227). The work is found incorporated, in other manuſcripts, with the *Politicus* of Benedictus and with the *Liber Cenſuum* of Cencius Camerarius; and De Roſſi has pointed out the importance of this circumſtance, not only as bearing upon the queſtion of its age, but alſo as ſhowing that the *Mirabilia* was about the end of the twelfth century inſerted as a quaſi-official document among the books of the Roman Curia.*

The copies of the *Mirabilia* above referred to exhibit the text in what is regarded as its original form; and it ſhould be obſerved that the earlier copies have no general title. The name placed upon the title-page of this volume is that which was applied to the book in the fourteenth and fifteenth centuries, and by which it has ſince been generally known.

It appears ſhortly after its production to have undergone a reviſion by another hand, which produced a work conſiderably altered by additions, omiſſions, and rearrangement of parts. This recenſion of the *Mirabilia* is diſtinguiſhed among critics by the name of *Graphia*, becauſe, in a manuſcript of the thirteenth or

* De Roſſi, *Roma Sotterranea*, i. 158.

fourteenth century, preferved in the Laurentian Library at Florence, it is found with the title, *Graphia aureae urbis Romae*.

With refpect to the date of the compofition of the *Mirabilia*, we find in the ftatements of the book itfelf the following indications, which limit its epoch in one direction. In both forms of the work, the porphyry farcophagus of the emperor Hadrian is defcribed as being at that time the tomb of Innocent II. who died 1143, and its cover as being in the Parvife of Saint Peter over the prefect's tomb (p. 79). The prefect has been identified by Gregorovius with the prefect Cinthius or Cencius, who died 1079. Of a ruin in the Forum, poffibly the temple of Julius, it is faid in the earlier work, that it is now called the Tower of Cencio Frangipane (p. 99). This well-known leader in the party warfare of Rome flourifhed in the early years of the twelfth century.

In the *Graphia* the following references occur, which are not in the original work. The farcophagus of the emprefs Helena is faid to have been converted into the tomb of pope Anaftafius IV., who died 1154 (p. 79); and there is mention of a houfe then belonging to the fons of Pierleone (p. 112). Pierleone, father of pope Anaclete II., died in 1128.

It is evident, from thefe paffages, that the *Mirabilia* in its earlieft exifting form is not older than the middle of the twelfth century, to which period it is attributed by fome of the beft authorities.

Another indication of date fhould be mentioned, which however is fomewhat in controverfy. The fecond, third, and fourth chapters of the third Part coincide with two fections of the Hiftory of the Bafilica of Saint Peter by Petrus Mallius, a work dedicated to pope Alexander III. (1159—1181);[*] and the queftion arifes, to which of the two

---

[*] Printed in the 27th volume of the *Acta Sanctorum*.

books thefe paffages originally belonged. This queftion is difcuffed by Jordan (*Topographie Roms* ii. 360, 426), who maintains that Mallius borrowed from the *Mirabilia*, while others have affumed the converfe to be true. In any cafe, it appears that the *Mirabilia* fhould be affigned either to the middle, or to the latter half, of the twelfth century, fince the age of the earlier manufcripts fhows that the work was in exiftence about the clofe of that period. Gregorovius, in an interefting account of the *Mirabilia*,* dwells upon the allufion to the Palace of the Senators and the Golden Capitol (pp. 86, 90) as evidence bearing on the age and fuggeftive as to the authorfhip of the book, which he imagines to have been compiled by fome one concerned in the revival of the Senate in 1143.

The *Graphia* appears to be of a date not much later than the original work.

* *Hiftory of Medieval Rome* (Ital. Tranfl.), iv. 356-384.

It is certainly as old as the thirteenth century, its antiquity being confirmed by the fact that Galvaneus Flamma, in a book written in or before 1297, and called *Manipulus Florum*, cites it as *liber valde authenticus*.* Martin of Troppau (Archbifhop of Gnefen, 1278), who completed his Chronicle of the World in 1268, afterwards added an introduction in which he made ufe of the *Mirabilia* in this form; and Fazio degli Uberti, in his poem called *Il Dittamondo*, written in the metre of the *Divina Commedia* between 1355 and 1367, devotes a canto to a defcription of Rome in which the poet is evidently largely indebted to the *Graphia*. It was in this form that the *Mirabilia* was known to the Englifh chronicler, Ranulf Higden, who has inferted long extracts from it in that part of the *Polychronicon* which relates to Rome. This work was edited, for the Hiftorical Series of the

* Muratori, *Scriptores*, xi. 540.

Master of the Rolls, by the late Rev. Churchill Babington, who printed with the Latin text two ancient English tranflations. It is worth while to obferve that Higden refers to the *Mirabilia Romae* as the work of a certain *Magifter Gregorius;* but the citations appear to be taken from a late revifion of the book, and the name of Mafter Gregory does not afford any ufeful clue to the original authorfhip.

The *Mirabilia* was firft printed in recent times by Montfaucon in 1702, in the *Diarium Italicum*. The manufcript ufed was then in the Convent of S. Ifidoro at Rome, and the text appears to be that of the *Graphia* in a late and fomewhat enlarged fhape.

In its older form the *Mirabilia* was firft printed in 1820 (from a manufcript attributed to the 13th century, then in the Barberini Library) in three feveral parts of a work called *Effemeridi Litterarie di Roma* (vol i. p. 62-82,

147-167, 378-392), with a preface figned by Count Alberti, and with anonymous annotations in Italian, which appear to have been the work of Nibby. This edition was reprinted, with the notes, in a fmall volume in 12mo. (Roma, dalla topografia Forenfe, 1864).

The *Mirabilia* was included in two collections of documents publifhed in the fame year in Germany and France (Gräffe, *Beitrage zur Litteratur und Sage des Mittelalters*, Drefden, 4to. 1850, and Ozanam, *Documents inédits pour fervir à l'hiftoire litéraire de l'Italie*, 8vo. Paris, 1850). I have not feen thefe collections, but I conclude from the references to them in the editions of Parthey and Urlichs, that the former contains the *Mirabilia* in its older form, the latter the *Graphia*.

In 1857, the *Mirabilia* was again printed in Germany, in Papencordt's *Gefchichte der Stadt Rom im Mittelalter*, edited by Höfler. The text is that of Montfaucon, fide by fide with another derived from a manuscript at Prague, which appears to belong to the older form of the work.

In 1869, Dr. Guftaf Parthey printed the *Mirabilia* at Berlin, in a convenient finall 8vo. volume. His work was the refult of a comparifon of the text of Montfaucon with feveral manufcripts in the Vatican Library, and with the editions of Alberti and Ozanam. It gives the text of the *Graphia* in a very late form, with fome additions found only in one of the Vatican manufcripts.

Profeffor Henry Jordan, in 1871, publifhed the fecond volume of his valuable *Topographie der Stadt Rom in Alterthum*, which contains, at the end, a critical edition of the *Mirabilia*, and in the text a review of its origin and hiftory, and a commentary on its contents. In his edition of the text Prof. Jordan has taken great pains to diftinguifh the original compofition from the early recenfion, and from the additions fubfequently made.

In the same year Professor Charles Lewis Urlichs published his learned and useful *Codex Urbis Romae Topographicus*, in which he has included the *Mirabilia* in various successive forms. The first form, which is entitled by the editor *Descriptio plenaria totius urbis*, is what we have described as the original work; the title being taken from one of the Vatican manuscripts already referred to, in which it appears to be applied to the portion of the book called in the English translation the Third Part. The second form is that of the *Graphia*. The third, which he entitles *de mirabilibus civitatis Romae*, resembles the text of Montfaucon. The fourth is the *Mirabilia breviata et interpolata* of the fifteenth century. The fifth is the *Mirabilia cum renascente doctrina coniuncta;* and the sixth is a work founded on the *Mirabilia*, and written apparently by a Canon of St. Peter's between 1410 and 1415, which was printed by Lewis Merklin in 1852, and is commonly cited by the name of *Anonymus Magliabecchianus*, having been transcribed from a manuscript of the 15th century, which has the arms of Medici at the end, and is preserved in the Magliabecchian library at Florence.*

The English translation here printed contains the original *Mirabilia*, arranged for the most part in its original order;† but the additions of the *Gra-*

---

* Another copy of this work, which appeared to me more carefully written (about the close of the 15th century), is in the Library of St. Mark at Venice. MSS. Lat. cl. x. cod. 231.

† The only deviations from the order of the original copies are these: The chapter on the Columns (Part I. c. 10) which is found in those copies among the legends in the second Part, is placed among the kindred matter of the first Part, and the chapter on Holy Places (Part I. c. 12) is placed at the end of the first part, instead of preceding that on Bridges. A chapter on the Officers of the Imperial court, which in some of the earlier copies is inserted in the second part, is omitted (see p. 42). It is not found in the Vatican manuscript to which the first rank has been assigned.

phia are introduced into the text, and also such of the later additions of the fourteenth and fifteenth centuries as appear to enhance the value of the work. But in order that the student may, without the necessity of referring to the Latin editions, distinguish the different parts of the composition, the additions belonging to the *Graphia* are marked by the following signs † ✝, and those of later copies by brackets, thus [ ].

The division into chapters is found in several of the manuscripts, but not carried through so completely as it is in the Translation. The larger division into Parts is not expressly marked in any of the Latin copies, but is essential to the arrangement of the matter. Professor Jordan, was, I believe, the first to point out that the work in its original form consisted of three distinct portions; first, a list of principal objects of interest arranged under various heads; secondly, a collection of legends associated with

Roman monuments; and thirdly, a fort of perambulation of the ancient city, beginning at the Vatican, and ending in the Traftevere. In the *Graphia* and later recenfions, owing to their deviation from the original arrangement, this divifion was loft.

Of the notes which have been added, I need not fay, that they have no pre tenfion to be a complete commentary on the *Mirabilia*. Such a work would occupy a much larger fpace. They are intended rather to anfwer the firft queftions which arife in the mind of the reader to whom the fubject is not familiar, upon almoft every line of this treatife. In their compilation the author has been very largely indebted to the labours of his lamented friend, Profeffor Henry Jordan, who devoted a confiderable part of the fecond volume of his valuable work on Roman Topography, left unfinifhed at his premature deceafe, to the illuftration of the *Mirabilia*.

At the end of the English verſion of the *Mirabilia* the editor has appended ſome other tranſlations which have a ſpecial intereſt in connection with that work. This ſupplement of *Mirabiliana* confiſts of the five following articles.

I. A deſcription of the marvels of the Roman churches compiled in the year 1375. The Latin original of this piece is incorporated in one of the Vatican manuſcripts of the *Mirabilia* (Cod. Vat. 4265), and has been printed by Parthey in his edition; but it cannot be properly treated as a part of that work, from which indeed it differs in ſpirit and intention. It will be found, however, an intereſting ſupplement to it. As the ſtudent of the *Mirabilia* may imagine himſelf following an enthuſiaſtic ſcholar of the twelfth century around the claſſical antiquities of the city, then exerciſing a new attraction in the firſt dawn which preceded the revival of learning, ſo when he reads this ſupplement, he will feel that he has put himſelf under the guidance of a more old-fashioned cicerone, who in a later generation recalls the traveller's attention to the ecclefiastical marvels which had for so many centuries aroused the curiosity and awe of the ordinary pilgrim.

II. A description of Rome extracted from the Itinerary of the Hebrew traveller, Benjamin of Tudela. This too short description, contemporary with the *Mirabilia*, sets before the reader the aspect in which Rome appeared to the Jewish Rabbi of that period.

III. Extracts from the *Ordo Romanus* contained in the *Politicus* of Canon Benedict. It has been already mentioned that this work is found in ancient manuscripts associated with the *Mirabilia*. The passages which describe the processional routes are of essential importance in the interpretation of that book, and enable us to fix with some approach to certainty the position of many ruins mentioned in it without sufficient indication of their site. The manifeft predilection for pagan ruins and claffical names, fhown by a writer on ecclefiaftical ritual, is a moft ftriking proof of that renewed intereft felt by the learned of the twelfth century in the remains of antiquity, out of which the *Mirabilia* had its origin.

IV. Three documents bearing on matters mentioned in the *Mirabilia*. Two of them are Bulls of Popes; the third is the Lift of Relics preferved in the Lateran Bafilica, infcribed on a mofaic table of the thirteenth century, now fufpended in the new cloifter of that church. Thefe documents may ferve as examples of the two claffes of records,—legal inftruments and infcriptions,—which furnifh the moft truftworthy evidence upon medieval hiftory and topography. The two Bulls are the beft witneffes to the condition of the Capitol and of part of the Forum in the time of the *Mirabilia*, and the lift of relics fupplies the moft interefting commentary on the chapter relating to the basilicas founded by Constantine (Part. ii. c. 8), and upon the fourth chapter of Church Marvels in the first part of the Supplement.

V. At the end of the volume will be found a medieval map of Rome, of which a more detailed account forms the last article of the *Mirabiliana*; at the close of which is a short description of the Frontispiece.*

* The Editor takes this opportunity of setting right some errors and omissions in his printed pages.

In page 2, note 3, for *Forum of Nerva* we should read, *a monument adjoining the Forum of Nerva;* and the reference should be to *Mirabiliana,* p 161, n. 365. The *Arca Noe* is not mentioned in the *Mirabilia.*

In p. 65, n. 115, it should be added, that the eighth chapter, which is not in the original *Mirabilia,* is mainly taken from the History of the Basilica of St. Peter by Petrus Mallius; and in p. 73, n. 133, that chapters 2, 3, and 4 coincide with two sections (§ 127, 130) of the same book. See before p. xii.

In p. 110, note 230 should be read, *See p.* 93, *note* 187.

I have only to add my thanks to the friends who have encouraged me in the preparation of this little work, among whom it is an honour to me to mention the Commendatore John Baptift de Roffi, the higheft authority upon the medieval and ecclefiaftical antiquities of Rome, and Profeffor Charles Lewis von Urlichs of Würzburg, whofe name has been fo long and honourably affociated with the fubject of Roman topography. It will be readily feen that this volume owes much to the publifhed works of both thefe archæologifts.

CONTENTS

PART I.

Of the Foundation of Rome, and of her chief monuments.

Chapter 1. Of the Foundation of Rome - - 1
2. Of the Town Wall - - - 6
3. Of the Gates - - - - 6
4. Of Triumphal Arches - - - 9
5. Of the Hills - - - - 16
6. Of Thermae - - - - 17
7. Of Palaces - - - - 19
8. Of Theatres - - - - 23
9. Of Bridges - - - - 24
10. Of the Pillars of Antonine and of Trajan, and of the Images that were of old time in Rome - - - 25
11. Of Cemeteries - - - - 26
12. Of places where Saints suffered - 29

PART II.

Divers Hiſtories touching certain famous Places and Images in Rome.

Chapter 1. *Of the Viſion of Octavian, and of the Sibyl's Anſwer* - - - 35
2. *Of the Marble Horſes, and of the Woman encompaſſed with Serpents* - 39
3. *Wherefore the Horſe was made that is called Conſtantine's* - - - 42
4. *The making of the Pantheon, and of its Conſecration* - - - 46
5. *An Homily of Saints Abdon and Sennen, Sixtus and Laurence* - 50
6. *Wherefore Octavian was called Auguſtus, and wherefore was dedicated the church of Saint Peter at the Chains* - - - - - 57
7. *Of the Coloſſeum, and of Saint Silveſter* - - - - - 62
8. *Of the Foundation of the three great Churches of Rome by Conſtantine, and of his parting from Pope Silveſter* 65

PART III.

A Perambulation of the City.

Chapter 1. Of the Vatican, and the Needle - 70
2. Of the Bafin, and Golden Pinecone in Saint Peter's Parvife - - 73
3. Of the Sepulchre of Romulus and the Terebinth of Nero - - - 75
4. Of the Caftle of Crefcentius or Memorial of Hadrian - - - - 78
5. Of the Sepulchre of Auguftus - - 80
6. Of divers places between the Sepulchre of Auguftus and the Capitol - - 82
7. Of the Capitol - - - - 86
8. Of the Palace of Trajan and his Forum, and of the Temples nigh thereto - - - - - 91
9. Of the Temple of Mars by the Prifon of Mamertinus, and of other buildings nigh to Saint Sergius his Church - 94
10. Of Cannapara, and the place called Hell, and of the Temples between Cannapara and the Arch of Seven Lamps - - - - - 96
11. Of the Palatine Hill and the parts nigh thereto - - - - 101

12. Of the Circus of Tarquin - - 103
13. From the Caelian Hill to Saint Cross in Jerusalem - - - - 106
14. Of the Eastern Quarter of the City - 107
15. Of the parts of the City nigh unto the Tiber - - - - - 110
16. Of the Transtiberim - - - 115
17. Conclusion - - - - - 117

MIRABILIANA.

PART I.

The Marvels of Roman Churches.

Chapter 1. Of the Founding of the Church of Saint Mary Major - - - 121
2. Of the Conversion of Constantine - 122
3. Of the Basilica of Saint Peter - 125
4. Of the Church of Lateran - - 129
5. Of Saint Paul's Basilica, and the Cloister of Anastasius - - - 133
6. Of Saint Mary Major and Round Saint Mary - - - - 134
7. Of Saint Mary New - - - 135

8. Of divers Churches and Relics - 137
9. Of Pope Joan - - - - 139
10. Of Ara Celi and Saint Sixtus - 141
11. Of the things beyond Saint Sixtus - 142
12. Of the Palatine and Saint Gregory 143
13. Of sundry Churches and Relics - 144
14. Of the Churches in Transtiberim - 148
15. Of the Aventine Hill - - - 148
16. Of Saint Barbara, Saint Martin, and Saint Agnes - - - 149
17. Of Saint Laurence - - - 151
18. Of Saint Sebastian - - - 151

PART II.

A description of Rome by Benjamin of Tudela, an Hebrew Traveller, about A.D. 1170 - - - - 153

PART III.

Ordo Romanus.

Extract 1. *Procession from Saint Anastasia to the Vatican* - - - - 157
2. *Procession from Saint Hadrian to Saint Mary the Greater* - - 160

Extract 3. Procession from Saint Mary the Greater to the Lateran, with the Ceremony of the Laſt Supper - 163
4. Procession from the Lateran to Saint Peter's and back - - - 165
5. Procession from the Coloſſeum to Saint Peter's - - - - - 172
6. Procession with the Sacred Picture on the Feaſt of the Aſſumption - 173

PART IV.

Three Records.

1. Grant of the Capitoline Hill by Anaclete II. to the Abbey of Saint Mary in the Capitol - - - 176
2. Grant of half the Arch of Severus and other property by Innocent III. to the Church of Saint Sergius and Bacchus 179
3. Table of Relics at the Lateran Baſilica. Engliſh Tranſlation - 182
Literal Copy of the ſame Table - 186

PART V.

Deſcription of the Medieval Plan of Rome at the end of the Volume; and of the Frontiſpiece - - - - 187

INDEX - - - - 197

ILLUSTRATIONS.

Part of a Bas-relief on the Bronze Door
    of Saint Peter's -   -   Frontiſpiece.
Medieval Map of Rome   -   At page 196.

THE MARVELS OF ROME.

Part I.

Of the Foundation of Rome; and of her Wall, Gates, Arches, Hills, Thermae, *Palaces, Theatres, Bridges, Pillars, Cemeteries, and Holy Places.*

1. *Of the Foundation of the City of Rome.*[1]

† AFTER the sons of Noah built the Tower of Confusion, Noah with his sons entered into a ship, as

---

[1] This chapter belongs to the Graphia, or second recenfion of the *Mirabilia*; the additions of which are diftinguifhed by the figns ††. See Preface. It has no fpecial value, except to fill up our conception of the nafcent archæology of the thirteenth century. It will be feen, that Varro is exprefsly referred to; and other authorities may be readily recognifed.

Hefcodius[2] writeth, and came unto
Italy. And not far from the place
where now is Rome, he founded a city
of his own name;[3] wherein he brought
his travail and his life to an end. Then
his fon Janus, with Janus his fon, Japhet
his grandfon, and Camefe a man of the
country, building a city, Janiculum, in
the Palatine mountain, fucceeded to the
kingdom; and when Camefe had gone
the way of all flefh, the kingdom paffed
to Janus alone. The fame, with the
aforefaid Camefe, did build him a palace
in *Tranftiberim*, that he called Janiculum, to wit, in that place where the
church of Saint John at Janiculum now
ftandeth.[4] But he had the feat of his

---

[2] An author named Efcodius, or Eftodius (otherwife unknown), is cited by Martinus Polonus in the
prologue to his Chronicle, by Johannes Caballinus,
De virtutibus Romanorum, and by other medieval
authors Urlichs, *Codex Romae Topographicus*, 113,
139; Graf, *Roma nel Medio Evo*, i. 66.

[3] The writer had probably in mind *area Noe*, the
popular name of the Forum of Nerva. See Part
iii. chapter 8; Urlichs, *Codex*, 140, 225.

[4] This church appears to have been the fame as

kingdom in the palace that he had builded in the mountain Palatine; wherein all the Emperors and Cæsars of after times did gloriously dwell. Moreover at that time Nembroth, which is the fame as Saturnus that was fhamefully entreated of his fon Jupiter,[5] came to the faid realm of Janus, and upholden by his aid founded a city in the Capitol, which he called Saturnia after his own name. And in thofe days king Italus with the Syracufans, coming to Janus and Saturnus, built a city by the river Albala, and called it after his name; and the river of Albula they did name Tiber, after the likenefs of the dyke of Syracufe that was fo called. After this, Hercules coming unto the realm of Janus with the Argives, as Varro telleth,[6] made a city called Valentia

St. John *in mica aurea*. Its exact fite is not known. See chapter 7, note 43.

[5] The myth alluded to belongs to the preceding generation of Gods. Hefiod. *Theog.* 179.

[6] The paffage in Varro relates to the Sacraria Argeorum. *Argeos dictos putant a principibus, qui cum*

under the Capitol. And afterwards, Tibris, king of the Aborigines, coming with his nation did build him a city by the Tiber, nigh whereunto he was flain by Italus in a fight that he had with him. At laft Evander, king of Arcady, with his men made a city in the Palatine mountain.[6] In like wife Coribas, coming with an hoft of Sicanians, built a city faft by, in the valley. And Glaucus alfo, younger fon of the fon of Jupiter,[7] coming thither with his men, raifed a city and built walls. After whom Roma, Aeneas' daughter, coming with a multitude of Trojans, built a city in the palace of the town.[8] Moreover Aventinus Silvius,[9] king of the Albans,

Hercule Argivo venerunt Romam, et in Saturnia fub-federunt. Varro, *L.L.* chapter 45.

[6] Virgil, *Aen.* viii. 51, 319, 330.

[7] *Filius minor eius filii Iovis.*

[8] *Veniens Romæ filia Hence . . civitatem in palatio urbis conftruxit.*

[9] This double name is taken from Varro, fupplemented by Livy. *Aventinum . . (dictum) a rege Aventino Albano.* Varro, *L. L.* 43. *Manfit Silviis poftea omnibus cognomen qui Albae regnaverunt.* Liv. i. 3.

did rear him a palace and maufoleum in the mountain Aventinus.

Now when the four hundred and thirty-third year was fulfilled after the deftruction of the town of Troy, Romulus was born of the blood of Priam, king of the Trojans. And in the twenty-fecond year of his age, in the fifteenth day of the Calends of May, he encompaffed all the faid cities with a wall, and called the fame Rome after his own name. And in her Etrurians, Sabines, Albans, Tufculans, Politanes, Telenes, Ficanians,[10] Janiculans, Camerians, Capenates, Falifcans, Lucanians, Italians, and, as one may fay, all the noble folk of the whole earth, with their wives and children, come together for to dwell.†

---

[10] *Ancus* . . (Politorio capto) *multitudinem omnem Romam traduxit* . . . *Additi eodem, Tellenis Ficanaque captis, novi cives.* Liv. i. 33.

2. *Of the Town Wall.*[11]

THE wall of the city of Rome hath towers three hundred threescore and one, castles forty and nine, [chief arches seven,] battlements six thousand and nine hundred, gates twelve, posterns five; and in the compass thereof there are twenty and two miles, without reckoning the *Transtiberim*, and the Leonine city, [that is the same as Saint Peter's Porch.]

3. *Of the Gates.*[12]

THE gates of the famous city be these. *Porta Capena*, that is called Saint Paul's Gate, by the Temple

---

[11] Very full and curious particulars concerning the matters referred to in this section are found at the end of the Einsiedeln Itinerary. (Urlichs, *Codex Topog.* 78; Jordan, *Topographie*, ii. 578.) There is no mention there of *castles* or *chief arches*. The exaggeration of the circuit of wall, which is common to other medieval descriptions, is thought by De Rossi to have originated in a misapprehension of the measurements given by Pliny. *Hist. Nat.* iii. 5, 66; De Rossi, *Piante di Roma*, 68.

[12] The gates are named in the order of their

of Remus;[13] *porta Appia*, [where is the church, that is named *Domine quo vadis*, that is to say, Lord whither goest thou, where are seen the footsteps of Jesus Christ]; *porta Latina*, [because there the Latins and Apulians were wont to go into the city; there is the vessel that was filled with boiling oil and in the which the blessed John the Evangelist was set]; *porta Metrovia*; *porta Asinaria*, that is called Lateran Gate; *porta Lavicana*, that is called Greater; *porta Taurina*, that is called Saint Laurence's Gate, or the gate of Tivoli, [and it is called *Taurina*, or the Bull Gate, because there be carved thereon two heads of bulls, the one lean and the other fat; the lean head, that is without,

position, beginning with the Porta di San Paolo, and ending with the *Porta Flaminia* (or Porta del Popolo), and the gate which closed the passage of the Ponte di Sant' Angelo.

[13] The pyramid of Cestius bore the name of Sepulchre (or Temple) of Remus, as the pyramid which formerly stood near the Castle of St. Angelo was called the Sepulchre of Romulus. See Part iii. chapter 1.

fignifieth them that come with flender fubftance into the city, the fat and full head within fignifieth them that go forth rich]; *porta Numentana* [that leadeth to the city of Nomentum]; *porta Salaria*, [the which hath two Ways, to wit, the old Salarian Way that leadeth to the Milvian Bridge, and the new way that goeth forth to the Salarian Bridge]; *porta Pinciana*, [becaufe king Pincius his palace is there][14]; *porta Flaminia*, [that is called Saint Valentine's];[15] *porta Collina*, at [the caftle that is by Saint Peter's bridge, the which is called the emperor] Hadrian's caftle, [who made Saint Peter's bridge].

Beyond Tiber be three gates: *porta*

---

[14] A *domus Pinciana* exifted in a ruinous condition in the time of Theodoric. Caffiodorus (*Var.* iii. 10) gives the form of an order for the removal to Ravenna of fome of its marble materials. Nothing more is known of its hiftory. Confiderable remains appear in the medieval plans.

[15] The ancient church of St. Valentine, repaired by Leo III. (795—816), was outfide the Porta del Popolo, near Ponte Molle.

Septimiana, seven Naiads joined with Janus;[16] *porta Aurelia* or *aurea*, that is to say, Golden [the which is now called Saint Pancras his gate]; and *porta Portuenfis*.

[In Saint Peter's Porch be two gates, whereof the one is called the gate of the Castle of the holy Angel, and the other *porta Viridaria*, that is to say, the gate at the Garden].[17]

4. *Of Triumphal Arches.*

ARCHES Triumphal be these that follow [the which were made for an Emperor returning from a triumph,

---

[16] *Septem Naiades iunctae Iano*. These words, which were suggested by Ovid (*Metam*. xiv. 785), appear to be introduced to supply an etymology for the name *Septimiana*. The later copies substitute the words *ubi septem laudes fuerunt factae Octaviano*.

[17] The *porta Viridaria* is now represented by Porta Angelica. The name was derived from the *viridarium* or garden, which was behind the Vatican Palace, and which was surrounded with a new wall by pope Nicolas III. in 1278. See an ancient inscription preserved in the Palace of the Conservators in the Capitol; and De Rossi, *Piante*, p. 83.

and whereunder they were led with worſhip by the ſenators, and his victory was graven thereon for a remembrance to poſterity]; Alexander's Golden Arch at Saint Celſus,[18] the arch of the emperors Theodoſius and Valentinian and Gratian at Saint Urſus;[19] the triumphal arch [of marble that the Senate decreed to be adorned with trophies in honour of Druſus, father of Claudius Caeſar, on account of the Rhætic and German wars by him nobly atchieved; whereof the veſtiges do barely appear] without the Appian Gate at the temple of Mars; in the Circus the arch of Titus and Veſ-

---

[18] The marble arch, which was at Saint Celſus under the church tower, is ſaid to have fallen down during the time of Pope Urban V. (1362-70). *Anonymus Magliabecchianus*, Urlichs, *Codex*, 153. Jordan identifies this arch with that of Arcadius, Honorius and Theodoſius, of which the inſcription is preſerved in the Einſiedeln Itinerary. *Topographie*, ii. 413.

[19] The church of Saint Urſus was near the bridge of Saint Angelo. The *Anonymus* ſpeaks of the arch as whole, but not of marble. Urlichs, *Codex*, 153.

pafian;[20] the arch of Conftantine by the Amphitheatre; at New Saint Mary's, between the Greater Palace and the temple of Romulus, the arch of the Seven Lamps of Titus and Vefpasian, [where is Mofes his candleftick having feven branches, with the Ark, at the foot of the Cartulary Tower]; the arch of †Julius† Caefar and the Senators between the *Aedes Concordiae* and the Fatal Temple, [before Saint Martina, where be now the Breeches Towers];[21] nigh unto Saint Laurence *in Lucina*, the triumphal arch of Octavian;[22] An-

---

[20] The infcriptions of an arch *in via Appia* in honour of Auguftus, and of an arch *in circo maximo* in honour of Titus, have been preferved in the Einfiedeln Itinerary. The added words refpecting the former arch are of the fifteenth century.

[21] The arch of Severus probably gained the name here given to it from a careleſs reading of the infcription, ftill preferved upon it, IMP. CAES. . . . S. P. Q. R. It was crowned in the Middle Ages by two towers, one of which belonged to the church of SS. Sergius and Bacchus. Hence the name, *turres de Bracis*. Nichols, *Notizie dei Rostri*, 63, 65.

[22] The fite of this arch, which croffed the *via Flaminia*, is marked by an infcription on the houfe,

toninus his arch, nigh to his pillar, [where is now the tower of the Tofetti].[23] Then there is an arch at Saint Mark's, that is called Hand of Flefh,[24] †for at the time when in this city of Rome, Lucy, an holy matron, was tormented for the faith of Chrift by the emperor Diocletian, he commanded that fhe

No. 167 Corfo, at the corner of the Via della Vite. Its attribution to Octavian is purely arbitrary. It is now generally believed to have been erected in honour of Marcus Aurelius; and fome of its fculptures are in the Mufeum of the Confervators.

[23] This was probably the Arch of Claudius. which carried the *Aqua Virgo* acrofs the *Via Flaminia* in front of the Palazzo Sciarra, and which bore an infcription commemorating the Emperor's campaign in Britain. The name of Antoninus was borrowed from the neighbouring column. The furname of the Tofetti occurs elfewhere; the pofition of their Tower is not known.

[24] *Arcus manus carneae* is mentioned in a Proceffional Order of the twelfth century, as lying between St. Mark's and the *Clivus Argentarius*. This Order is extracted in a future page. The name Macel dei Corvi, ftill exifting in this locality, is thought to be derived from it. This name (*Macellum corvorum*) is given in Bufalini's plan to the Salita di Marforio.

should be laid down and be beaten to death; and behold, he that smote her was made stone, but his hand remained flesh, unto the seventh day; wherefore the name of that place is called Hand of Flesh to this day.²⁵† In the Capitol is the arch of Gold Bread;²⁶ [and in the Aventine the arch of Fauſtinus nigh to Saint Sabina.²⁷

There are moreover other arches, which are not triumphal but memorial

---

²⁵ The ſtory told in the text is found in the medieval *Acta S. Luciae.* Mombritius, *Acta Sanctorum,* ii. 60.

²⁶ *Arcus panis aurei.* The Graphia has *arcus aureus.*

²⁷ Nothing is, I think, known of this arch. It is curious that the arch of Severus at Saint George *in Velabro* is omitted. The *Anonymus* mentions it at the end of his longer liſt (Urlichs, *Codex,* 156). The great double arch, near, was probably converted into a tower. The arch of Severus, which is partly under the corner of the campanile, may have been incloſed by other buildings. An inſcription preſerved in the apſe of the church records, that in the year 1259 Cardinal Peter Capocci gave to the church three ſites adjoining the campanile, *tres ſitas iuxta turrim dicte ecclesie que dicitur adcavallarañ, ita quod dicte terre aliquo titulo alienari non poſſint.*

arches, as is the arch of Piety before Round Saint Mary's.[28] In this place upon a time, when an emperor was ready in his chariot to go forth to war, a poor widow fell at his feet, weeping and crying: Oh my lord, before thou goeſt, let me have juſtice. And he promiſed her that on his return he would do her full right; but ſhe ſaid: Peradventure thou ſhalt die firſt. This conſidering, the emperor leapt from his chariot, and held his conſiſtory on the ſpot. And the woman ſaid, I had one only ſon, and a young man hath ſlain him. Upon this ſaying the emperor gave ſentence. The murderer, ſaid he, ſhall die, he ſhall not live. Thy ſon then, ſaid ſhe, ſhall die, for it is he

---

[28] The arch of Piety before St. Mary *in Aquiro*, is mentioned in Part iii. chapter 6; and St. Mary *in Aquiro* is deſcribed in a Proceſſional Order as being *ad arcum Pietatis*. See *Ordo Romanus*, Extract 1, further on. De Roſſi has conjectured that the widow of the legend was, in the original ſculpture, a ſuppliant nation at the feet of an emperor.

that playing with my son hath slain him.
But when he was led to death, the
woman sighed aloud, and said, Let the
young man that is to die be given unto
me in the stead of my son; so shall I be
recompensed, else shall I never confess
that I have had full right. This therefore was done, and the woman departed
with rich gifts from the emperor.][29]

[29] The legend of the Justice of Trajan, and of
St. Gregory being moved by the sculpture to obtain
the admission of the heathen emperor to Paradise,
is as old as the eighth century. It is told by Paulus
Diaconus in his Life of Gregory; and it appears
to have found especial favour in England, being
related by Iohannes Diaconus in the next century,
as read in the English churches (*Acta SS. Ord.
Bened.* i. 395, 425), and also by John of Salisbury,
a contemporary of the *Mirabilia* (*Polycraticus*, l. 5,
c. 8). In the original story the sculpture was seen
by St. Gregory in the Forum of Trajan; but when
this was destroyed, the legend migrated to another
monument upon which an appropriate sculpture was
found. The history of the legend is discussed by
Graf, *Roma nel Medio Evo*, ii. cap 12. In the
Mirabilia the narrative is secularized by the omission
of the part of Gregory, and complicated by the
additional facts of the culprit being the son of the
emperor and being saved by the intercession of his

5. *Of the Hills.*

HILLS within the city be thefe: *Janiculus* [that is commonly called Janarian, where is the church of Saint Sabba]; Aventine, that is alfo called Quirinal [becaufe the Quirites were there, where is the church of Saint Alexius]; Cælian [where is the church of Saint Stephen *in monte Caelio*]; Capitol [or Tarpeian hill, where is the Senator's palace[30]]; *Pallanteum* [where

---

accufer. Dante found the fame fubject carved in Purgatory.

> Quivi era floriata l'alta gloria
>   Del Roman prince, lo cui gran valore
> Moffe Gregorio alla fua gran vittoria:
>   Io dico di Traiano imperadore:
> Ed una vedovella gli era al freno
>   Di lagrime atteggiata e di dolore.
> Dintorno a lui parea calcato e pieno
>   Di cavalieri; e l'aquile nell' oro
> Sovra effo in vifta al vento fi movieno.
>
> *Purgatorio*, x. 73.

[30] The Senate was reftored in name in 1143, and inftalled in the Capitol, probably in the ancient Tabularium. See Gregorovius, *Hiftory of Rome in the Middle Age* (Ital. tranfl.), iv. 519, 550. De Roffi has called attention to a document dated

is the Greater Palace]; Exquiline [that is called above others,[31] where is the bafilica of Saint Mary the Greater]; Viminal [where is Saint Agatha's church, and where Virgil, being taken by the Romans, efcaped invifibly and went to Naples, whence it is faid, *vado ad Napulim.*][32]

6. *Of Thermae.*[33]

THERE be called *thermae* great palaces, having full great crypts under ground, wherein in the winter-

---

1150, *in capitolio in confiftorio novo palatii.* Chron. Pifan. Muratori, vi. 171.

[31] *Qui fupra alios dicitur.* See Part iii. c. 14.

[32] The medieval fame of Virgil as a wizard has been difcuffed in feveral recent works. See efpecially Genthe, *Leben und Fortleben des Virgilius;* Comparetti, *Virgilio nel Medio Evo.*

The words, *vado ad Napulim,* allude to the name *Balneapolis,* given to the ruins on the eaft fide of the Forum of Trajan. (Jordan, *Topographie,* ii. 310.) In a lift of churches of the fourteenth century it is written *Varionapolis* (Urlichs, *Codex,* 171.) The name ftill furvives in the Via Magnanapoli.

[33] Of the ten *thermae* here named, the following fix are identified with *thermae* named in the Notitia:

time a fire was kindled throughout, and in fummer they were filled with frefh waters, fo that the court dwelt in the upper chambers in much delight; as may be feen in the *thermae* of Diocletian, before Saint Sufana]. Now there are the Antonian Thermae; the Domitian *Thermae;* the Maximian; thofe of Licinius; the Diocletian; the Tiberian [behind Saint Sufana]; the Novatian; thofe of Olympias [at Saint Laurence *in panifperna*]; thofe of Agrippa [behind Round Saint Mary's]; and the Alexandrine [where is the hofpital of the *Thermae*].

Antonianae (*Antoninianae*), *Domitianae* (*Traianae*, see *Lib. Pontif. Symmachus*, 33), *Licinii* (*Surae*, or *Licinii Surae*), *Diocletianae, Agrippianae, Alexandrinae.* The Novatian are known in ecclefiaftical ftory. (*Acta S. Praxedis*, 19 Mai, p. 295). *Thermae Tiberianae* and *Maximianae* are perhaps names of other ruins (not public baths). The Tiberian are faid by the *Anonymus* to be behind S. Sufana broken down by age, probably in the garden of Salluft. Compare the *palatium Tiberii*, in Part iii. c. 14. The *Thermae Salluftianae* occur in the Einfiedeln Itinerary, and appear to have been the real fcene of the martyrdom of St. Laurence. *Acta S. Laurentii*, 10 Aug. p. 519.

7. Of Palaces.[34]

PALACES in the city be these: the Greater Palace †of the Monarchy of the Earth, wherein is the capital seat of the whole world, and the Cæsarean palace †, in the Pallantean hill;[35] †the palace of Romulus nigh unto the hut of Faustulus;† the palace of Severus [by Saint Sixtus]; the palace of Claudius [between the Colosseum and Saint Peter *in vincula*]; the palace of Constantine [in the Lateran, where my lord Pope dwelleth]: †this Lateran palace was Nero's, and named from the side of the northern region wherein it standeth, or from the frog which Nero secretly pro-

---

[34] This term is evidently applied, not only to the genuine palaces of popular and ecclesiastical tradition, but to other important ruins. The explanations of locality, added in the later copies to the bare list of names given in the older *Mirabilia*, cannot always be taken as a true interpretation of the original meaning.

[35] The remains of the imperial palaces on the Palatine were called, throughout the Middle Age, *palatium maius*.

duced;[35] in the which palace there is now a great church †; the Sufurrian palace † where is now the church of Saint Crofs†;[36] the Volufian palace; the palace of Romulus [between New Saint Mary and Saint Cofmas], where are the two temples of Piety and Concord,[37] and where Romulus fet his golden image,

[35] *Dictum a latere feptentrionalis plagae in quo fitum eft, vel a rana quam Nero latenter peperit.* The ftory of Nero's parturition is told by Matthew of Weftminfter, and other medieval writers. See Graf, i. 338-345.

[36] The *Bafilica Sefforiana*, founded by St. Helena, and enriched with relics brought by her from Jerufalem, had the name of Jerufalem. *Palatium quod appellatur Sefforium* exifted in the time of Theodoric. (*Excerpta Valefiana,* apud Ammianum, ed. Gardthaufen, ii. 298.) The Einfiedeln traveller, going eaftward acrofs the ruined city, paffed, firft, *palatium iuxta iherufalem*, and then, *Hierufalem*. (*Itin. Einfied.*; Urlichs, *Codex*, 73.) The Volufian palace, next mentioned, was probably named, not from the emperor, but from a Volufian affociated in legend with the ftory of Pilate. Graf, i. 380, 392.

[37] The palace or temple (thefe words in Mirabi¹ian nomenclature are frequently interchanged) of Romulus was the Bafilica of Conftantine. The temple of Piety and Concord was the double temple of Venus and Rome. See Part iii. c. 10.

saying, It shall not fall till that a virgin bear a child; and as soon as the Virgin bore a son, the image fell down;[38] the palace of Trajan and Hadrian, where is the pillar [twenty paces of height]; Constantine's palace;[39] Sallust his palace; Camillus his palace;[40] Antonine's palace, where is his pillar [twenty-seven paces high]; Nero's palace[41] [where is Saint Peter's Needle] †and wherein rest the bodies of the

[38] A like story is told by Alexander Neckam (*De naturis rerum*, ed. Wright, p. 312), as a supplement to the story of the Vision of Augustus (see further on, Part ii. c. 1); but it is Virgil who uses the words, *It shall not fall*, &c. of the palace of Augustus.

[39] This second palace of Constantine was probably the *thermae Constantinianae* on the Quirinal. See Part iii. c. 14.

[40] *Palatium Camilli*, otherwise *Camillanum* (Part iii. c. 6.), and *Campus Camilianus*, was the site of the ancient monastery of SS. Cyriac and Nicolas, now apparently absorbed in the convent of S. Marta (founded 1546), near the Collegio Romano. An arch, called *Arcus Camilli*, crossing the Via del Piè di Marmo at the north-west corner of the convent, is shown in Bufalini's plan, dated 1502.

[41] The original *Mirabilia* ends the chapter with the words *Palatium Neronis, ubi est sepulchrum Julii*

Apoſtles Peter and Paul, Simon and Jude; Julius Cæſar's palace, where is the ſepulchre of Julius Cæſar; Chromatius his palace; Eufimianus his palace; the palace of Titus and Veſpaſian without Rome at the catacombs;[42] Domitian's palace beyond Tiber at the Golden Morſel†;[43] Octavian's palace [at Saint Laurence *in Lucina*].[44]

Caeſaris: palatium Octaviani. The later copies have ſome of the additions of the Graphia (diſtinguiſhed in the text by the croſſes ††), and add *palatium Pompeii* after *Chromatii.* As to the *palatium Chromatii,* ſee Part iii. c. 15.

[42] In the deſcription of Rome by the Jewiſh traveller, Benjamin of Tudela, the palace of Titus is outſide the walls. See the extract at the end of this volume.

[43] *Palatium Domitiani in tranſtiberim ad micam auream.* A place called *mica aurea* occurs in the Einſiedeln Itinerary (Urlichs, *Codex,* 73); and is apparently in the Traſtevere. And a church of St. John *in mica aurea* on the Janiculum occurs in the fourteenth century. (See note 4; Gregorovius, *Hiſtory,* Ital. tranſl. iii. 636; Urlichs, *Codex,* 175.) Perhaps it is the ſame as Montorio, a name ſaid to be derived from the yellow ſand found there.

[44] *Palatium Octaviani* in the original text probably alludes to the legend of Ara cœli (ſee Part ii. c. 1) the later addition to the arch mentioned in p. 11.

8. *Of Theatres.*[44]

THE theatres be these: the theatre of Titus and Vespasian at the catacombs; the theatre of Tarquin and the Emperors at the Seven Floors; Pompey's theatre at Saint Laurence [*in Damaso*]; Antoninus his theatre by Antoninus his bridge; Alexander's the-

---

[44] The first six monuments named under this head appear to be the following: 1, the circus of Maxentius, 2, the Circus Maximus, 3, the theatre of Pompey, 4, the theatre of Balbus, 5, the stadium of Severus Alexander (Piazza Navona), 6, the circus of Hadrian near the mausoleum of Hadrian. The seventh and last monument may be the Circus Flaminius. But if this interpretation is correct, not only the Colosseum, which might seem to form a class by itself, but the theatre of Marcellus is omitted. There is some reason to suspect that the latter building is denoted by the term *Theatrum Flaminium*. When the remains of the Flaminian circus had become obscure, the name may have been transferred to the more conspicuous ruin. See at the end of cap. 12; and see also the first extract from the Ordo Romanus at the end of this volume. In the medieval Acts of St. Agnes, the prefect comes *ad theatrum*, that is, to the Alexandrine stadium. Mombritius, f. 18.

atre nigh unto Round Saint Mary's; Nero's theatre nigh to Crescentius his castle; and the Flaminian theatre.

9. *Of Bridges.*[45]

BRIDGES be these: the Milvian bridge; the Hadrian bridge; the Neronian bridge †at *Saffia*†;[46] the Antonine bridge †*in arenula*†,[47] the Fabrician bridge, †which is called the Jews' bridge†, [because Jews dwell there]; Gratian's bridge †between the island and the *Transtiberim*†; the Senators' bridge †of Saint Mary†;[48] the marble bridge of Theodosius †at

---

[45] The bridges are arranged in order, going down the stream.

[46] The locality now called Borgo di San Spirito in Saffia was in the early Middle Age known as the *Vicus Saxonum* or *Saxonia*, owing to the foundation there of a *Schola Saxonum* by Ini, king of the West Saxons, in 727, and of a hospital for pilgrims by Offa, king of Mercia, in 794.

[47] *Pons Antoninus*, the *Pons Aurelius* of the Notitia, the modern Ponte Sisto in the region called Arenula; broken down before 1018, rebuilt 1475.

[48] The Ponte Rotto, called St. Mary's Bridge from the church of St. Mary Egiziaca.

the Riparmea†, and the Valentinian bridge.[49]

10. *Of the Pillars of Antonine and of Trajan; and of the Images that were of old time in Rome.*[50]

THE winding pillar of Antonine[51] hath one hundred threescore and fifteen feet of height, steps in number two hundred and three, windows forty and five. The winding pillar of Trajan hath in height one hundred thirty and eight feet, steps in number one hundred fourscore and five, windows forty and five.

The coloſſean Amphitheatre hath one hundred and eight ſubmiſſal feet of height.[52]

---

[49] *Riparmea* ſhould, according to Jordan, be *Ripa Romea*, a medieval name for the Ripa Grande. The ſame author thinks that the Valentinian Bridge was the ſame as that of Theodoſius, and that there were never more than two bridges below the iſland. *Topographie*, ii. 195.

[50] The materials of this ſection are derived from the Notitia.

[51] *Columpna Antonini coclidis*.

[52] *Coloſſeum Amphitheatrum* (*Coloſſus amphitheatri*,

†In Rome were twenty and two great horses of gilded brass, horses of gold fourscore, horses of ivory fourscore and four,⁵³ common jakes an hundred and fourscore and four, great sewers fifty, bulls, griffons, peacocks, and a multitude of other images, the costliness whereof seemed beyond measure, insomuch that men coming to the city had good cause to marvel at her beauty.†

11. *Of Cemeteries.*⁵⁴

THE cemeteries be these; the cemetery of Calepodius at Saint Pancras; the cemetery of Saint Agatha at

---

Graphia). The Notitia, in the fourth region, mentions *Colossum altum pedes centum duo semis.* After the removal of the statue, the name of Colossus passed to the amphitheatre. The word *submissales* (for which I do not know that any meaning has been suggested) seems to have arisen out of the *semis* of the Notitia.

⁵³ In the Notitia it is *Dei aurei LXXX. eburnei LXXXIIII.* By careless transcription the gods have been changed to horses.

⁵⁴ Before the eleventh century, the insecurity of the open country had led to the abandonment of the ancient cemeteries or catacombs, and to the

the Ring;[55] Urſus his cemetery at Portefa;[56] Saint Felix his cemetery; Calixtus his cemetery by the catacombs [at the church of Saint Fabian and Saint Sebaſtian]; Prætextatus his cemetery nigh unto the Appian gate at Saint Apollinaris; Gordian's cemetery without the Latin gate; the cemetery between Two

---

removal of the venerated remains of ſaints and martyrs to the churches within the walls. De Roſſi has ſhown that this ſection is topographically arranged, and founded upon information which would not have been acceſſible to a writer of the eleventh century, unleſs he copied from an older written work (De Roſſi, *Roma Sotterranea*, i. 158, 175-183). William of Malmeſbury has a valuable account of the cemeteries arranged under the names of the gates leading to them, which is evidently copied from ſome good earlier authority. Will. Malmeſb. *de Geſtis reg. Angl.* ed. Savil, 1601, p. 135.

[55] *Ad girolum.* This cemetery was near the Porta di S. Pancrazio. The *girolus* was the circus of Caligula. The name Agatha may have been ſuggeſted by Agapita, the name of a ſaint buried there.

[56] There has been a tranſpoſition of names. It ſhould be, The cemetery of the Capped Bear (*urſi pileati*) in the Via Portuenſis, and the cemetery of Urſus at S. Viviana, within the walls. De Roſſi, *Roma Sotterranea*, i. 175-183.

Bays[57] at Saint Helen's; the cemetery of the Capped Bear[58] at Saint Viviana; the cemetery of the *ager Veranus* at Saint Laurence [without the walls]; the cemetery of Saint Agnes; the cemetery of Saint Peter's well;[59] Prifcilla's cemetery at the Salarian bridge; the cemetery at the Cucumber Hill;[60] Trafo's cemetery at Saint Saturninus; the cemetery of Saint Felicity nigh unto that of Calixtus; [the cemetery of Saint Marcellus on the old Salarian Way; the cemetery of Balbina on the Ardeatine Way; the cemetery of the Innocents at Saint Paul]; the Pontian cemetery; the

---

[57] *Inter duos lauros.* The burial-place of St. Helen, on the Via Labicana.

[58] *Cimiterium urfi pileati.* See note 56.

[59] *Cimiterium fontis* [al. *ad nympham*] *fancti Petri.* The *fons S. Petri* was on the Via Nomentana, where St. Peter was faid to have baptized. De Roffi, *Roma Sotterranea*, i. 159, 179.

[60] *Cimiterium clivi cucumeris.* The oldeft copies have *cimiterium cucumeris.* The fpot, *locus qui dicitur cucumeris*, is defcribed by William of Malmefbury as near the point where the *Via Pinciana* joined the *Via Salaria.* Will. Malmefb. ed. Savil, 1601, p. 135.

cemetery of Saint Hermes and Domitilla; the cemetery of Saint Cyriac on the Oſtian way. [Theſe cemeteries were chambers under ground that ſometimes ſtretched for three miles, and wherein the holy martyrs were hidden.]

12. *Of places where Saints ſuffered.*[61]

THESE are the places that are found in the paſſions of Saints: without the Appian gate, the place where the bleſſed Sixtus was beheaded, and the place where the Lord appeared to Peter, when he ſaid, Lord, whither goeſt thou, and the temple of Mars;[62]

---

[61] Profeſſor Jordan (*Topographie*, ii. 380) has ſupplied moſt of the references to the Acta Sanctorum, which I give below. See alſo Mariinelli, *Roma Sacra*, 37.

[62] The temple of Mars, about two miles from the Porta Appia, was the place where St. Sixtus was beheaded. *Acta S. Sixti*, 6 Aug. 140. See alſo *Acta S. Stephani*, 2 Aug. 141; *S. Cornelii*, 14 Sept. 144. In the legendary Acts of Pope Stephen (Mombritius, ii. 274) the temple fell upon the prayer of that ſaint.

within the gate, the Dripping Arch;[63] then, the region of Fafciola at Saint Nereus;[64] the *Vicus Canarius* at Saint George, where was Lucilla's houfe,[65] and where is the Golden Vail;[66] the *aqua Salvia* at Saint Anaftafius, where the bleffed Paul was beheaded, [and the head thrice uttered the word Jefus, as it bounded, and where there be yet three wells which fpring up diverfe in tafte];[67] the garden of Lucina, where

[63] *Intra portam arcus ftillae.* The fo-called Arch of Drufus, which carried an aqueduct acrofs the road. St. Stephen Pope was imprifoned and held a Synod *in carcere ad arcum ftellae*, perhaps not the fame place. (*Lib. Pontif. Steph. I.*) A fcholiaft to Juvenal gives the name *arcus ftillans* to the Porta Capena on account of the aqueduct over it. *Schol. ad Juv.* iii. 11.

[64] *Felix III. Renaxus de titulo Fafciolae. Lib. Pontif.* in vita Felicis III.

[65] *Acta S. Laurentii*, 10 Aug. 518; *S. Eufebii*, 25 Aug. 115; *S. Sixti*, 6 Aug. 141.

[66] *Eft ibi velum aureum*, the medieval corruption of *Velabrum;* another corrupted form occurs in the infcription cited in Note 27.

[67] The church of St. Anaftafius at the Tre Fontane was given by Innocent II in 1140 (about the

is the church of the blessed Paul, and where he lieth.[68] *Interlude*, that is, between two Games;[69] the hill of Scaurus, which is between the Amphitheatre and the Racecourse, before the Seven Floors,[70] where is the sewer, wherein Saint Sebastian was cast, who

date of the Mirabilia) to Saint Bernard, who founded there a convent of Cistercian monks.

[68] More correctly the Cemetery of Commodilla. De Rossi, *Roma Sotterr.* i. 185; *Acta Sanctorum*, Juni. vol. vii. 488.

[69] *Interlude, id est inter duos ludos.* A few lines below we find: *in tellure, id est in cannapara*. (See also Part iii. c. 10). The locality called *in Tellure*, or *locus Telluris* (also *in Tellude* and *Telludis templum*), occurs frequently in Acts of Saints and elsewhere, as the place where the Praefectus Urbis held his tribunal. *Lib. Pontif.* Cornelius, 5; *Acta S. Gordiani*, 10 Mai. 551; *S. Crescentiani*, 16 Ian. 370, 372; *S. Marii*, 19 Ian. 580; *S. Stephani*, 2 Aug. 142; *S. Sixti*, 6 Aug. 141; *S. Abundii*, 16 Sept. 301. The temple of Tellus was near the Suburra, *in Carinis*. *Corp. Inscr. Lat.* i. 145.

[70] *Circus Scauri, qui est inter amphitheatrum et stadium* (between the Colosseum and the Circus Maximus) was the residence of Saint Gregory, where the church of Saint Gregory now stands. Near this was the *Septizonium Severi*, called, in Mirabilian nomenclature, *septemsolium* or *septem solia*.

revealed his body to Saint Lucina, faying Thou fhalt find my body hanging on a nail;[71] the *via Cornelia* by the Milvian bridge, and goeth forth into the ftreet;[72] the *via Aurelia* nigh to the Ring;[73] the fteps of Eliogabalus in the entry of the Palace;[74] the chained ifland behind Saint Trinity;[75] the Dripping Arch before the Seven Floors;[76] the Roman Arch between the Aventine and Albifton, where the bleffed Silvefter and Conftantine kiffed, and departed the one from the other;[77] *in Tellure*, that is the *Canapara*,

---

[71] The words are taken from the Acts of St. Sebaftian (20 Ian. 642). *Sebaftianus apparuit S. Lucinae dicens, in cloaca illa quae eft iuxta circum invenies corpus meum pendens in gompho.*

[72] *Et exit in ftratam.* The meaning is obfcure.

[73] *Iuxta girolum*, the Circus of Caligula, near the Vatican.

[74] *Gradus Eliogabali.* (*Acta S. Sebaftiani*, 20 Ian. 642.) The locality appears to have been on the Palatine Hill.

[75] *Et infula catenata poft fanctam Trinitatem.*

[76] *Arcus stillans ante septemfolium.* See Notes 63, 70.

[77] *Albifton* was a name given to the church of St. Balbina; see Part iii. c. 11. The legend of the parting of Conftantine and Saint Silvefter, when

where was the houfe of Tellus;[78] the prifon of Mamertinus before the Mars under the Capitol;[79] the *Vicus Latericii* at Saint Praxede; the *Vicus Patricii* at Saint Pudentiana;[80] the bafilica of Jupiter at Saint Quiricus;[81] the *thermae* of Olympias, where the bleffed Laurence

the Emperor was fuppofed to have furrendered Rome with the fupremacy of the Weftern Empire to the Pope, was of great political importance. See Part ii. c. 8; Gregorovius, *Hiftory*, Ital. tranfl. iv. 405; Graf, ii. 98.

[78] The Canapara appears to have been in the ruins of the Bafilica Julia (see Part iii. c. 7), whereas the ancient temple of Tellus was in the quarter called *Carinae*. See Note 69.

[79] *Privata Mamertini*. The ancient *Carcer*, and the traditional prifon of the apoftles Peter and Paul; oppofite to which was the ftatue of a river-god, mifcalled Mars, more lately Marforio. *Privata Mamertini* occurs in the *Acta S. Stephani Papae*. Mombritius, ii. 274.

[80] *Vicus latericius* occurs only in connection with the church of St. Praxede. *Vicus patricius* was an ancient ftreet, and was famous in ecclefiaftical tradition for the houfe of Pudens and the refidence of St. Peter.

[81] *Bafilica Iovis* is mentioned in the Acts of St. Laurence as a part of the Palace of Tiberius (*Acta S. Laurentii* 10 Aug. 518). It is placed here at St.

was broiled, in Panifperna;[82] the Tiberian palace of Trajan, where Decius and Valerian withdrew themfelves after Saint Laurence's death,[83] [where the place is called the Baths of the Cornuti;][84] the *Circus Flaminius* at the Jews' bridge;[85] in the *Tranftiberim*, the temple of the Ravennates, pouring forth oil, where is Saint Mary's.[86]

Quiricus. Compare Part iii c. 8. In a Proceffional Order the name occurs near the Piazza Montanara. See the firft extract from the *Ordo Romanus*.

[82] The thermae of Olympias are not named in the Acts of St. Laurence. See Note 33, *ad fin.*

[83] *Acta S. Laurentii*, 10 Aug. 518.

[84] *Thermae de Cornutis* (al. *cormitiis*).

[85] *Acta S. Marcelli*, 16 Ian. 371. The 'Flaminian Circus at the Jews' Bridge' was perhaps the Theatre of Marcellus. See p. 23, Note 44; and *Ordo Romanus*, Extract 1.

[86] See Part iii. c. 16.

Part II.

The Second Part containeth divers Histories touching certain famous Places and Images in Rome.

1. *Of the Vision of Octavian the Emperor, and of the Sibyl's Answer.*[87]

IN the time of the emperor Octavian, the Senators, seeing him to be of so

---

[87] The legend of Augustus and the prophecy of Christ first occurs in the *Chronographia* of Malalas, a writer according to Gibbon (*Hist.* c. xl. note 11) little later than Justinian, who died in 565. (Malalas, *Chronog.* lib. x. p. 231, ed. Dindorf.) This Greek form of the legend is given more concisely by Suidas. "Augustus Cæsar, after he had sacrificed, asked the Pythia who should reign after him, and she said:

> An Hebrew Child, that rules among the Blessed,
> Bids me forego my house, and seek the shades.
> Thou therefore henceforth from my shrine depart.

And, going forth from the oracle, Augustus set in the Capitol an altar, on which he inscribed, in Latin letters, This is the Altar of the First-born great beauty, that none could look into his eyes,[68] and of so great prosperity and peace, that he had made all the world to render him tribute, said unto him: We desire to worship thee, because the godhead is in thee; for if it were not so, all things would not prosper with thee as they do. But he, being loth, demanded a delay, and called unto him the Sibyl of Tibur, to whom he rehearsed all that the Senators had said. She begged for three days space, in the which she kept a straight fast; and thus made answer to him after the third day: These things, sir emperor, shall surely come to pass:

> Token of doom : the Earth shall drip with sweat ;
> From Heaven shall come the King for evermore,
> And present in the flesh shall judge the world.

God." (Suidas, *Lexicon*, s. v. Αἴγουστος.) The history of the legend is very fully discussed by Graf, *Roma nel Medio Evo*, i. 309—320.

[68] *Forma fuit eximia . . . oculos habuit claros ac nitidos . . gaudebatque si quis acrius intuenti, quasi ad fulgorem solis, vultum dimitteret.* Suetonius, *Augustus*, c. 79.

And the other verses that follow.[89] And anon, †whiles Octavian diligently hearkened to the Sibyl,† the heaven was opened, and a great brightness lighted upon him; and he saw in heaven a virgin, passing fair, standing upon an altar, and holding a man-child in her arms, whereof he marvelled exceedingly; and he heard a voice from heaven †saying, This is the Virgin that shall conceive the Saviour of the World. And again he heard another voice from heaven,† saying, This is the altar of the Son of God. The emperor straightway fell to the ground, and worshipped the Christ that should come. This vision he showed to the Senators, and they in like wise marvelled exceedingly. The vision took place in the chamber of the emperor

[89] *Iudicii signum, Tellus sudore madescet :
E caelo Rex adveniet per secla futurus,
Scilicet in carne praesens ut iudicet orbem.*

These three lines are the first of twenty-seven, given by Saint Augustine, as a translation from a Greek poem ascribed to the Erythræan Sibyl. *De Civitate Dei*, l. xviii. c. 23.

Octavian, where now is the church of Saint Mary in the Capitol, [where the Friars Minors are.][90] Therefore is it called Saint Mary *in ara cœli*.[91]

†Upon another day, when the people had decreed to call him Lord, he forthwith ſtayed them with hand and look, neither did he ſuffer himſelf to be called Lord even by his ſons,[92] saying:

<blockquote>Mortal I am, and will not call me Lord.†</blockquote>

---

[90] The Franciſcans were eſtabliſhed in 1250, twenty-five years after St. Francis' death, in the Abbey of the Capitol, where they ſtill retain a feeble hold on the church.

[91] The proper name of the church continued until the thirteenth century to be *Sancta Maria in Capitolio*. (Gregorovius, *Hiſtory*, Ital. tranſl. iv. 545.) Jordan ſuggeſts that the authority of the Mirabilia may have led to the official recognition of the name connected with the legend. *Topographie*, ii. 366.

[92] Theſe facts are derived fron Suetonius (*Auguſtus*, c. 53), and repeated, as having a religious ſignificance, by Oroſius, *Hiſt*. lvi. c. 22.

2. Of the Marble Horses,[93] and of the Woman encompassed with Serpents.

HEAR now to what intent the Horses of marble were made bare, and the men beside them naked, and what story they tell, and what is the reason why there sitteth before the horses a certain woman encompassed with serpents, and having a shell before her.

In the time of the emperor Tiberius there came to Rome two young men that were philosophers, named Praxiteles and Phidias, whom the emperor, observing them to be of so much wisdom, kept nigh unto himself in his palace; †and he said to them, wherefore do ye go abroad naked? who answered and said: Because all things are naked and open to us, and we hold

---

[93] The legend of Phidias and Praxiteles, and that which follows in the next chapter, of the Brazen Horse, are evidently stories which had their origin upon the spot, out of the fancy of pilgrims, or of their guides.

the world of no account, therefore we go naked and poſſeſs nothing;† and they ſaid: Whatſoever thou, moſt mighty emperor, ſhalt deviſe in thy chamber by day or night, albeit we be abſent, we will tell it thee every word. If ye ſhall do that ye ſay, ſaid the emperor, I will give you what thing ſoever ye ſhall deſire. They anſwered and ſaid, We aſk no money, but only a memorial of us. And when the next day was come, they ſhowed unto the emperor in order whatſoever he had thought of in that night. Therefore he made them the memorial that he had promiſed, to wit, the naked horſes, which trample on the earth, that is upon the mighty princes of the world that rule over the men of this world; and there ſhall come a full mighty king, which ſhall mount the horſes, that is, upon the might of the princes of this world. Meanwhile there be the two men half naked, which ſtand by the horſes, and with arms raiſed on high and bent fingers tell the things that are to be; and as they be naked,

The Woman with Serpents. 41

so is all worldly knowledge naked and open to their minds. The woman encompaffed with ferpents, that fitteth with a fhell before her, [fignifieth the Church, encompaffed with many rolls of fcriptures],[94] to whom he that defireth to go, may not, but if he be firft wafhed in that fhell, [that is to fay, except he be baptized].[95]

---

[94] The words here added are found only in the edition of Montfaucon. The earlier manufcripts are imperfect in this paffage, and inftead of the claufe in brackets, have only the words *praedicatores qui praedicaverunt eam*.

[95] Of the female fitting ftatue, which appears from this paffage to have been on the Quirinal in front of the Marble Horfes, nothing further is known. I have fome fufpicion that its remains may be found in the coloffal fitting Hygieia of the Giuftiniani Palace, remarkable for the large folds of the ferpent furrounding the figure. Thefe folds, without their reftored head, might be taken for feveral ferpents. Of the prefent figure the knees and part of the ferpent are original, perhaps not much elfe. See Matz, *Antike Bildwerke in Rom*, i. 227; *Galleria Giuftiniani*, plate 8; Clarac, *Mufée de Sculpture*, No. 890.

G

3.[96] *Wherefore the Horse was made, that is called Constantine's.*

THERE is at the Lateran a certain brazen horse, that is called Constantine's Horse;[97] but it is not so, for

---

[96] Some of the earlier copies have a section in this place upon the officers of the imperial court, which has been omitted, having no relation to the subject of the *Mirabilia*. See Urlichs, *Codex*, 97.

[97] There seems to be some reason for thinking that the bronze statue of Marcus Aurelius, which was before the Lateran Palace as early as the tenth century, and was known as the Horse of Constantine, was the same statue which had been before called by the same name in the Forum, and which appears to have been still there in the ninth century. (*Itin. Einsiedeln.* Urlichs, *Codex*, 71.) De Rossi suggests, that in the decay of art as evidenced by the use of the Trajan sculptures in the arch of Constantine, a statue of Marcus Aurelius may have been dedicated by the Senate to Constantine. There is no actual proof of identity, beyond the disappearance of the name in one place and its appearance in the other. The statue at the Lateran, according to Ranulf Higden, was called by pilgrims Theodoric, by the people Constantine, and by the clergy Marcus, or Quintus Curtius; and he tells a story similar to that given in the text, of a knight called Marcus. Higden, *Polychronicon*, ed. Babington, i. 228.

whofoever will know the truth thereof, let him read it here.

In the time of the Confuls and Senators, a certain full mighty king from the parts of the Eaſt came to Italy, and befieged Rome on the fide of the Lateran, and with much flaughter and war afflicted the Roman people. Then a certain fquire of great beauty and virtue, bold and fubtle, arofe and faid to the Confuls and Senators: If there were one that fhould deliver you from this tribulation, what would he deferve from the Senate? and they anfwered and faid: What thing foever he fhall afk, he fhall prefently obtain it. Give me, faid he, thirty thoufand fefterces, and ye fhall make me a memorial of the victory, when the fight is done, and a horfe in gilded brafs of the beſt. And they promifed to do all that he afked. Then faid he, Arife at midnight and arm you all, and ſtand at watch within the walls, and whatfoever I fhall fay to you, that fhall ye do. And they forthwith did that he bade them. Then he mounted an horfe without a faddle, and took a fickle. For he had feen of many nights the king come to the foot of a certain tree for his bodily need, at whofe coming an owlet, that fat in the tree, always hooted. The fquire therefore went forth of the city and made forage, which he carried before him tied up in a trufs, after the fafhion of a groom. And as foon as he heard the hooting of the owlet, he drew near, and perceived that the king was come to the tree. He went therefore ftraightway towards him. The lords that were with the king, thought he was one of their own people, and began to cry, that he fhould take himfelf out of the way from before the king. But he, not leaving his purpofe for their fhouting, whiles he feigned to go from the place, bore down upon the king; and fuch was his hardihood that in defpite of them all he feized the king by force, and carried him away. Anon, when he was come to the walls of the city, he began to cry, Go forth and flay all the king's army, for lo! I have

taken him captive. And they, going
forth, flew fome and put the others to
flight; and the Romans had from that
field an untold weight of gold and filver.
So they returned glorious to the city;
and all that they had promifed to the
aforefaid efquire they paid and per-
formed, to wit, thirty thoufand fefterces,
and an horfe of gilded brafs without a
faddle for a memorial of him, with the
man himfelf riding thereon, having his
right hand ftretched forth, that he took
the king withal, and on the horfe's head
a memorial of the owlet, upon whofe
hooting he had won the victory. The
king, which was of little ftature, with
his hands bound behind him, as he had
been taken, was alfo figured, by way of
remembrance, under the hoof of the
horfe.[98]

[98] Montfaucon concluded from this paffage that
there was formerly the figure of a captive under the
ftatue (*Diarium Italicum*, 301). This conjecture
appears to find fome confirmation in another
legendary explanation of the work, according to
which it reprefented Conftantine trampling under

4. *Of the making of the Pantheon, and of its Confecration.*[99]

IN the times of the Confuls and Senators, the prefect Agrippa, with four legions of foldiers, fubjugated to the Roman fenate the Suevians, Saxons, and other weftern nations. Upon whofe return the bell of the image of the kingdom of the Perfians, that was in the Capitol, rang. For in the temple

---

his horfe's feet a dwarf, whom his wife had received as a lover. Enenkel, *Weltbuch*, cited by Graf, *Roma nel Medio Evo*, ii. 110. The bird is reprefented by a tuft of hair between the horfe's ears.

[99] This fection contains two legends, not neceffarily connected. The legend of the bells, known as *Salvatio Romae*, is at leaft as old as the eighth century, being narrated in Greek by Cofmas of Jerufalem (*Comment. ad S. Gregor. Nazianzen,* Mai. *Spiceleg. Rom.* ii. 221; Urlichs, *Codex*, 179), and in Latin in a book *De feptem mundi miraculis*, attributed to Bede, and found in a manufcript of that century. (*Bede's Works*, ed. Giles, iv. 10; Graf, *Roma nel Medio Evo*, i. 112, 189; fee alfo Jordan, *Topographie*, ii. 366.) The other legend, of Agrippa and Cybele, does not feem to be found in any earlier work.

of Jupiter and Moneta in the Capitol was an image of every kingdom of the world, with a bell about his neck, and as foon as the bell founded, they knew that the country was rebellious. The prieſt therefore that was on watch in his week, hearing the found of the bell, ſhewed the fame to the Senators; and the Senators did lay the ordering of this war upon the prefect Agrippa. He denying that he was of ability to undergo fo great a charge, was at length conſtrained, and aſked leave to take counfel for three days. During which term, upon one night, out of too much thinking he fell aſleep, and there appeared to him a woman, who faid unto him: What doeſt thou, Agrippa? forfooth, thou art in great thought; and he anſwered unto her: Madam, I am. She faid, Comfort thee, and promife me, if thou ſhalt win the victory, to make me a temple fuch as I ſhow unto thee. And he faid, I will make it. And ſhe ſhowed him in the viſion a temple made after that faſhion. And he faid: Madam, who art thou? And fhe faid, I am Cybele, the mother of the gods: bear libations to Neptune, which is a mighty god, that he help thee; and make this temple to be dedicated to my worfhip and Neptune's, becaufe we will be with thee, and thou fhalt prevail. Agrippa then arofe with gladnefs, and rehearfed in the Senate all thefe fayings; and he went, with a great array of fhips and with five legions, and overcame the Perfians, and put them under a yearly tribute to the Roman Senate. And when he returned to Rome, he built this temple, and made it to be dedicated to the honour of Cybele, mother of the gods, and of Neptune, god of the fea, and of all the gods, and he gave to this temple the name of Pantheon. And in honour of the fame Cybele he made a gilded image, which he fet upon the top of the temple above the opening, and covered it with a magnifical roof of gilded brafs.

After many ages pope Boniface, in the time of Phocas, a Chriftian emperor, seeing that so marvellous temple, dedicated in honour of Cybele, mother of the gods, before the which Christian men were ofttimes stricken of devils, prayed the emperor to grant him this temple, that as in the Calends of November it was dedicated to Cybele, mother of the gods, so in the Calends of November he might consecrate it to the blessed Mary, ever-virgin, that is the mother of all saints. This Cæsar granted unto him; and the pope, with the whole Roman people, in the day of the Calends of November did dedicate it; and ordained that upon that day the Roman pontiff should sing mass there, and the people take the body and blood of our Lord as on Christmas day;[100] and that on the same day all saints with their mother, Mary ever-virgin, and the heavenly spirits should have festival, and the dead

---

[100] The practice of administering the sacrament under both kinds to the laity continued in Rome as well as in England in the twelfth century. Mabillon, *Musæum Italicum*, tom. ii. *Comment. in Ord. Rom.* p. lxi.

have, throughout the churches of the whole world, a sacrifice for ransom of their souls.[1]

5. An Homily of the Passions of the Holy Abdon and Sennen, Sixtus and Laurence.[2]

WHAT man that will preach the passion of the Saints Abdon and Sennen, or of Saint Sixtus, Laurence, and the rest, on the one hand, as the Lesson hath told it,[3] regarding for what

---

[1] The Pantheon was consecrated by Pope Boniface IV. probably in the year 610 (*Lib. Pontiff*; Nibly, *Roma Mod.* i. 407). The day kept as the dedication day is the 13th of May; but the festival of the 1st of November (All Saints' Day) is believed to have been first celebrated in Rome as the Feast of the Blessed Mother of God and of all Martyrs, and by Gregory IV. made a general festival for the whole Church. Usuardus, *Martyrol.* in *Acta Sanctorum*, vol. 26; Baronius, *Martyrol. Rom.* 1 Nov.

[2] This chapter contains an half-historical, half-legendary narrative, which might serve, as the author tells us, as part of a sermon on the passion, either of Saints Abdon and Sennen, of Saint Sixtus, or of Saint Laurence.

[3] *Sicut dixit lectio.* The lives of the Martyrs

cause the emperor did them to death, may begin thus: A tempeſt having arisen under Decius, many Chriſtians were slain, while Galba had rule in the city of Rome;[4] or on the other, as out of the Roman ſtory, may thus begin and preach: There was a certain emperor, Gordian by name, whoſe ſtandard-bearer in his legions was Philip. This Philip was a Chriſtian,[5] and he ſlew his lord the emperor Gordian, and took the

were called legends (*legendæ*) becauſe they were intended to be read in the ſervices upon their feſtivals.

[4] The old *acta* of Abdon and Sennen begin their ſtory at this point. Petrus de Natalibus, *Vitæ Sanctorum*, f. 131; Mombritius, *Acta Sanctorum*, f. 6.

[5] The belief that the Emperor Philip, who had the glory of celebrating the Secular Games on the thouſandth anniverſary of Rome, was a Chriſtian, aroſe partly during his own life. See Gibbon, c. 16. In later times this emperor and his ſon, having both been put to death by "the pagan Decius," were regarded as martyrs for the faith; and Petrus de Natalibus devotes a chapter to the *Acta Sanctorum Philippi et Philippi imperatorum et martyrum* (*Vitæ Sanctorum*, f. 219 b). Moſt of the facts narrated in the text are repeated either in the Acts of theſe emperors or in thoſe of Saint Laurence. Ib. f. 140.

empire, with his fon. For he had a fon named Philip. Now among the fervants of the emperor Philip was a certain knight named Decius, an heathen man of Pannonia, which grew in favour with the emperor, by the good fame of his knighthood, and with the foldiers and Senate by his wit, prudence, and bounty; whom the emperor with the Senate made chief captain, with four legions, againſt a nation of the Weſt that was rebellious; and he went and made war upon them and overcame them in many battles. Upon his return, his foldiers in their rejoicing praifed him, and faid, Oh, if he were our emperor, all things would be well with us. And, being enticed by the foldiers' words, he confpired with them that he ſhould have the empire, and ſhould give them duchies and marches and counties, and honours at court, and the treafure of Philip. Now when Decius was come to the parts of Liguria, the emperor Philip had betaken him to Verona, and, hearing of his return, received him gracioufly,

But after that day was paſſed, the ſoldiers of Decius ſecretly took up arms as they had agreed with their emperor that was to be; and Decius at midday went to the emperor's court with a ſword hidden about him, and entering into his tent, he caſt forth the chamberlain, and drawing his ſword ſmote Philip between the noſe and the lip as he ſlept in his bed, and ſo did him to death. And anon he went forth and founded a ſignal, whereupon all his ſoldiers ran to meet him around the tent, as they had afore deviſed. Meanwhile Philip's ſoldiers, hearing that their lord was ſlain of Decius, took to flight; but being called back in their terror by Decius, who bade them not fly, but become his friends, they at the laſt did return to him, but rather from fear than from love.

Now when the younger Philip, that was at Rome, heard that Philip his father was done to death by Decius the pagan, he was afraid, and fled to the bleſſed Sixtus, pope of the Romans, saying, My lord Father, my father is dead, whom the impious Decius hath done to death; I befeech thee take my father's treafure and keep it hidden, and if I efcape that Decius flay me not, thou fhalt render it to me again, but if not, thou fhalt have it for the Church. Decius then came to Rome, and obtained the empire more by his valour than from any love that was borne him; and he began to feek Philip the younger, that was hidden away. At the laft, by great promifes and gifts, he found him, and flew him. Then he made fearch after the treafure of Philip, and fome men faid that Sixtus, the pope of the Chriftians, had it, others faid it was at Philippopolis in Grecia. And at this very feafon there came an embaffage from the ruler of Persia, faying that they of that land were rebellious; and the bell of the image rang.[6] Decius therefore having ordained Galba to be his vicar at Rome, carried with him his

[6] See p. 47.

son Decius and fought againſt the Perſians and overcame them all, and took Abdon and Sennen, as it is declared in the Lesson, whom he knew to be of right noble race, and brought them away chained in golden fetters;[7] and as he returned, he laid ſiege to Philippopolis. In the mean time a meſſage came from Rome, and brought him tidings that Galba was dead. So he left Decius, his ſon, there with a part of his hoſt, and led the reſidue to Rome, together with Abdon and Sennen. Now, when he was come to Rome, he aſked diligently after the treaſures of Philip, the which he had not yet been able certainly to find. And he ſlew those holy martyrs, the right noble Abdon and Sennen in the Amphitheatre.[8] And it

---

[7] *Pergit Romam* [Decius] *ſecum adducens beatiſſimos ſubregulos Abdon et Sennen catenis vinctos . . eoque nobiles eſſent ad ſpectaculum Romanorum. Acta SS. Addon et Sennen,* Mombritius, f. 6 b.

[8] According to the legend, Abdon and Sennen were taken to the Amphitheatre, before the image of the Sun, and commanded to ſacrifice to the idol. (See chapter 7.) They refuſed and ſpat on the

was shewed unto him, that Sixtus, bishop of the Christians, had the treasure of Philip; so he took him and afflicted him with many torments. And because he could not be certified by him touching the treasures, Valerian commanded that he should undergo the sentence of death. And, even as he was led to be beheaded, the blessed Laurence cried out and said: Holy Father, leave me not behind, for behold, I have expended thy treasures that thou didst put into my hands. Then the soldiers, hearing of the treasures, laid hands on the blessed Laurence before the Seven Floors in the New Way, and took him and delivered him to Parthenius the tribune: and the residue that followeth.[9]

---

image; and were afterwards put to death by gladiators in the Amphitheatre. P. de Natalibus, f. 131; Mombritius, f. 6 b.

[9] *Acta S. Laurentii.* P. de Natalibus, f. 139 b; Mombritius, ii. f. 50. Nothing is said in the *acta* about the locality of the taking of St. Laurence.

6. *Wherefore Octavian was called Augustus, and wherefore was dedicated the church of Saint Peter at the Chains.*[110]

WHEN Julius Cæsar was done to death of the Senate, his nephew Octavian assumed the empire; against whom arose Antony, his brother-in-law, whose sceptre had remained after Cæsar's death,[1] and strove, with much ado, to take from him the empire. Antony, therefore, putting away Octavian's sister, took to wife Cleopatra, queen of Egypt, mighty in gold and silver and precious stones and people. When, therefore, Antony and Cleopatra, with

---

[110] The church of St. Peter *ad vincula* was founded by Eudoxia, the wife of the Emperor Valentinian III., who is confounded in the legend with Eudoxia, the wife of Arcadius. The feast-day of the dedication of this church, the 1st of August, was anciently observed as a festival in memory of the death of Antony. 1 *Aug. Feriae ob necem Antonii. Fasti* in *Corpus Inscr. Lat.* i. 376.

[1] *Caius bajulus . . remanserat.*

a great array of ſhips and people, began to come againſt Rome, the news was brought to the city, and Octavian, with a mighty array, went and fought againſt them in Epirus. Thus a battle began; and the queen's ſhip, which was all gilded, began to give way. Antony, feeing the queen's ſhip give way, withdrew him too, and followed her to Alexandria, where he fell on his ſteel and died. After this Queen Cleopatra ſaw that ſhe was reſerved for a triumph; ſo ſhe decked her with gold and precious ſtones, and would have bewitched Octavian with her beauty, but ſhe could not. Finding herſelf ſcorned, ſhe went, decked as ſhe was, into her huſband's tomb, and put to her breaſts two aſps, which is a manner of ſerpent; and they ſo ſweetly ſucked that ſhe fell aſleep and died. Octavian took away vaſt ſums of money from that victory, and triumphed over Alexandria and Egypt and all the country of the East, and ſo victorious came back to Rome. The Senate, therefore, and all the Roman people received him with great triumph, and becaufe the victory was in the Calends of the month *Sextilis*, they gave him the name of Auguftus by reafon of the augment or increafe of the commonwealth, and decreed that every year in the Calends of Auguft (for fo they alfo called the month) the whole commonalty fhould have a feftival of gladnefs for that aforefaid victory, to the honour of Octavianus Cæsar Auguftus, and the whole city fhould rejoice and be glad in fo great a feftival.

This rite endured to the time of Arcadius, the hufband of Eudoxia, who, after his death, was left with her fon Theodofius of tender age, and did manly rule the empire, as though her hufband Arcadius had been yet alive. Moved by the fpirit of God, and for the welfare of the commonwealth, fhe went to Jerufalem, and vifited the venerable Sepulchre and other holy places. And whiles fhe was bufy with the affairs of the commonwealth, the provincial folk brought unto her huge gifts, among the which a certain Jew brought her the chains of the blessed apostle Peter, wherewith he was bound of Herod in prison under four quaternions. The sight of these chains gave the queen more joy than all her other gifts; and she bethought her, that they could not elsewhere be put in so condign a place as where the blessed Peter's body resteth in dust. Coming, therefore, to Rome in the Calends of August, she saw that ancient rite of heathendom yet full solemnly observed of the Roman people in the Calends of *Sextilis*, the which none of the pontiffs had been able to set aside. She therefore made suit to pope Pelagius and the Senators and the people, that the favour which she should ask might be granted to her; and they readily promised to allow it. The Queen therefore said: I do perceive, that ye give much thought to the Sextile holiday in reverence of the dead emperor Octavian for the victory which he won over the Egyptians; I pray you give me up the worship of the dead

emperor Octavian for the worship of
the heavenly Emperor, and his apostle
Peter, whose chains, lo! I have brought
from Jerusalem, and like as he delivered
us from Egyptian bondage, so may that
heavenly Emperor from the bondage of
demons. And I am minded to make a
church to God's honour and Saint
Peter's, and to set there these chains;
which church the Pope, our lord Apostolic, shall dedicate in the Calends of
August, and it shall be called Saint
Peter at the Chains, and there our lord
Apostolic shall yearly, in the same
church, sing solemn mass; and as Saint
Peter was loosed by the angel, so
may the Roman people depart with a
blessing, freed from their sins. This
proposal was heard by the people and
received with little favour, but was at
length accorded unto the prayer of
the Pope and Queen. She therefore
built the church, which my lord Pope
dedicated in the Calends of August,
like as the most Christian Empress had
devised; and there she set the afore-

mentioned chains of the blessed Peter, and the Neronian chains of the blessed Paul; that in this day of the Calends of Sextilis the Roman people may flock thither, and do reverence to the chains of the apostles Peter and Paul.

7. *Of the Colosseum, and of Saint Silvester.*[2]

THE Colosseum was the temple of the Sun, of marvellous greatnefs and beauty, difpofed with many di-

---

[2] This chapter is found in manufcripts of the fourteenth century. Ranulph Higden gives the following marvellous account of the Coloffus, or image of the Sun, which he fuppofes to have been brought from Rhodes. "This brazen ftatue, gilded with imperial gold, continually fhed rays through the darknefs, and turned round in even movement with the fun, carrying his face always oppofite to the folar body; and all the Romans, when they came near, worfhipped in token of fubjection. The which Saint Gregory deftroyed by fire, as he might not do fo by ftrength; and only the head and the right hand holding a fphere outlafted the fire, and they are now upon two marble pillars before the palace of my lord

verse vaulted chambers, and all covered with an heaven of gilded brafs,[3] where thunders and lightnings and glittering fires were made, and where rain was fhed through flender tubes. Befides this there were the Signs fuperceleftial and the planets *Sol* and *Luna*, that were drawn along in their proper chariots. And in the midft abode Phœbus, that is the god of the Sun, which having his feet on the earth reached unto heaven with his head, and did hold in his hand

---

Pope. And it is marvel, how the founder's craft hath fo informed the ftubborn brafs, that the hair feemeth foft to the fight and the mouth as though it were fpeaking." Higden, *Polychronicon*, ed. Babington, 1, 234. A coloffal head and hand are reprefented as lying before the palace of the Lateran in a plan of the thirteenth or fourteenth century publifhed by De Roffi (*Piante di Roma*, tav. 1). Benjamin of Tudela fpeaks of the Sampfon before the Lateran as if it were an entire ftatue. See among the Mirabiliana, further on. The bronze head formerly at the Lateran is believed to be that now in the court of the Palace of the Confervators.

[3] In fome of the early plans publifhed by De Roffi, the Coloffeum is reprefented with a dome in accordance with this fancy.

an orb, signifying that Rome ruled over the world.[4]

But after a space of time the blessed Silvester bade destroy that temple, and in like wise other palaces, to the intent that the orators which came to Rome, should not wander through profane buildings, but shall pass with devotion through the churches. But the head and hands of the aforesaid idol he caused to be laid before his Palace of the Lateran in remembrance thereof; and the same is now falsely called by the vulgar Samson's Ball. And before the Colosseum was a temple, where ceremonies were done to the aforesaid image.]

---

[4] The Colossus is transferred from the outside to the interior of the Amphitheatre, which is itself converted into a temple. In the ecclesiastical tradition it retained its true place (see note 108). So in the earlier Mirabilia, the Sun-temple is before the Colosseum (Part iii. c. 11). This is remembered at the end of the present chapter.

8. *Of the Foundation of the three great Churches of Rome by the Emperor Conſtantine, and of his Parting from Pope Silveſter.*[5]

†IN the days of Pope Silveſter, Conſtantine Auguſtus made the Lateran Baſilica, the which he comely adorned. And he put there the Ark of the Covenant,[6] that Titus had carried away from Jeruſalem with many thouſands of Jews; and the golden candleſtick having ſeven lamps with veſſels for oil. In the which ark be theſe things, to wit, the golden emerods, the mice of gold, the Tables of the Covenant, the rod of Aaron, manna, the barley loaves, the golden urn, the coat without ſeam, the reed and garment of Saint John

---

[5] This chapter is from a manuſcript of the thirteenth century, *Cod. Vat.* 636. Parthey, *Mirabilia*, 31.

[6] *Archam teſtamenti.* Hebrews, ix. 4; Exod. xxv. 22.

Baptift, and the tongs that Saint John the Evangelift was fhorn withal.[7] Moreover he did put in the fame bafilica a civory[8] with pillars of porphyry. And he fet there four pillars of gilded brafs, which the Confuls of old had brought into the Capitol from the Mars' Field, and fet in the temple of Jupiter.[9]

---

[7] *Domitianus iuffit . . crines capitis eius tonderi, ut inhonorabilis ab omnibus videretur.* (*Acta S. Iohannis*, Mombritius, f. 29.) Baronius has a note on the different *forcipes* ufed in the torments of martyrs. *Martyrologium*, Iuni 26.) As to the relics of the Lateran church, compare Ioh. Diaconus, in Mabillon, *Mus. Ital.* ii. 564; Panvinio, *Sette Chiefe*, 158; Crefcembeni, *Iftoria della Chiefa di S. Giovanni avanti Porta Latina*, pp. 134-149; Urlichs, *Codex*, 117; and the ancient table, preferved in the cloifter by the Sacrifty, of which a copy will be found in the Mirabiliana.

[8] *Ciborium*, a canopy of ftone or marble over an altar. Hence the word, *civery*, *civer*, or *severey* was ufed by Englifh architects for the compartment of a vault. Ducange, s. v. *Ciborium*; Parker, *Gloffary of Architecture*, s. v. *Severy*.

[9] The bronze columns are believed to be thofe which now are at the altar of the Sacrament. In the table mentioned in note 117, they are faid to have been brought from Jerufalem by Titus. Urlichs cites the following extract from Vatican

He made alfo, in the time of the faid pope and after his prayer, a bafilica for the Apoftle Peter before Apollo's temple in the Vatican.[120] Whereof the faid emperor did himfelf firft dig the foundation, and in reverence of the twelve Apoftles did carry thereout twelve bafkets full of earth. The faid Apoftle's body is thus beftowed. He made a cheft clofed on all fides with brafs and copper,[1] the which may not be moved, five feet of length at the head, five at the foot, on the right fide five feet, and on the left fide five feet, five feet above, and five feet below; and fo he inclofed the body of the bleffed Peter, and the altar above in the fafhion of an arch he

---

Manufcript 1984, *ad hift. mifc.* f. 54, in margine Auguftus, conqueror of all Egypt, took from the fea-fight many *roftra*, or fhips-beaks, therewith he made four molten pillars, that were afterward fet by Domitian in the Capitol; and which we fee to this day, as they were at a later time well ordered by the emperor Conftantine the Great in the Bafilica of Saint Saviour. Urlichs, *Codex*, 117.

[120] See p. 70, note 126.

[1] *Loculum ex omni parte ex ere et cupro conclufit.*

did adorn with bright gold.[2] And he made a civory with pillars of porphyry and pureſt gold. And he ſet there before the altar twelve pillars of glaſs[3] that he had brought out of Grecia, and which were of Apollo's temple at Troy. Moreover he did ſet above the bleſſed Apoſtle Peter's body a croſs of pure gold, having an hundred and fifty pounds of weight; whereon was written: *Conſtantinus Auguſtus et Helena Auguſta.*

He made also a baſilica for the bleſſed apoſtle Paul in the Oſtian Way, and did beſtow his body in braſs and copper, in like faſhion as the body of the bleſſed Peter.

The same emperor, after he was become a Chriſtian, and had made theſe churches, did alſo give to the bleſſed Silveſter a *Phrygium*,[4] and white horſes,

---

[2] *Ornavit superius altare ex fulvo auro archam* (read *arcuatim*).

[3] *Columpnas vitrineas.*

[4] *Frigium.* This word (or *regnum*) appears to be the proper term for what is now commonly called the Tiara. See Ducange, s. v. *Phrygium.*

and all the *imperialia* that pertained to the dignity of the Roman empire; and he went away to Byzantium; with whom the pope, decked in the same, did go fo far forth as the Roman Arch, where they embraced and kiffed the one the other, and fo departed.†[5]

[5] See p. 32.

Part III.

The Third Part containeth a Perambulation of the City.

1. *Of the Vatican, and the Needle.*

WITHIN the Palace of Nero[6] is the temple of Apollo, that is called Saint Parnel;[7] before which is the basilica that is called Vatican, adorned with marvellous mosaic and ceiled with gold and glass. It is therefore called Vatican because in that place the *Vates*,

---

[6] The remains of the Circus of Caligula at the Vatican were called the palace of Nero; and near this, according to ecclesiastical tradition, was a temple of Apollo. *Sepultus est* (S. Petrus) *via Aurelia in templo Apollinis iuxta locum ubi crucifixus est, iuxta palatium Neronianum in Vaticano, iuxta territorium Triumphale, in Calendas Julias.* Anastasius, *Lib. Pontif.*

[7] *Quod dicitur Sancta Petronilla.* The church of St. Parnel, or Petronilla, was a round building where is now the apse on the south side of St. Peter's. Martinelli, *Roma Sacra*, 384.

that is to say, the priests, sang their offices before Apollo's temple, and therefore all that part of St. Peter's church is called Vatican. There is also another temple, that was Nero's Wardrobe,[8] which is now called Saint Andrew; nigh whereunto is the memorial of Cæsar, that is the Needle,[9] where his ashes nobly rest in his *sarcophagus*, to

[8] *Quod fuit vestiarium Neronis.* The church of St. Andrew *in Vaticano* became the Sacristy of St. Peter's. Hence perhaps the idea of *Vestiarium*. Bunsen, *Beschreibung*, II. i. 39.

[9] *Memoria Caesaris, id est Agulia.* The obelisk was popularly called St. Peter's Needle, *acus*, or *agulia, S. Petri.* A careless reading of the dedicatory inscription to Augustus and Tiberius (the Latin letters referred to in the text),

DIVO . CAESARI . DIVI . IVLII . F . AVGVSTO
TI . CAESARI . DIVI . AVGVSTI . F . AVGVSTO
SACRVM

may have led to its being taken for a memorial of Cæsar. The word Agulia, or Guglia, was also suggestive of *Julia*, or *columna Julia*. Compare Suetonius, *Iulius*, 85, upon which the following narrative of the twelfth century was founded. *Columpnam ei solidam lapidis Numidici XX prope pedum in foro statuerunt, super quam tumulatus, quae et Iulia dicta est. Chron. S. Pantelconis,* apud Eccard, *Corpus Hist.* ii 695; Urlichs, *Codex,* 181.

the intent that as in his lifetime the whole world lay fubdued before him, even fo in his death the fame may lie beneath him for ever. The memorial was adorned in the lower part with tables of gilded brafs, and fairly limned with Latin letters;[130] and above at the ball, where he refts, it is decked with gold and precious ftones, and there is it written:

> Cæfar who once waft great as is the world,
> Now in how fmall a cavern art thou clofed.[1]

---

[130] *Et litteris latinis decenter depicta.* Before the prefent bronze ornaments of eagles and feftoons were added in 1723, the holes, to which ancient decorations had been attached, were vifible. (Fontana, *Obelifco*, p 8.) The bronze lions, which appear to fuftain the obelifk, are of the time of its removal under Sixtus V. But it was conftantly ftated before its removal that it refted on four bronze lions (Higden, *Polychron.* ed. Babington, i. 226; Petrarch, *Lit. Famil.* vi. 2); and Higden tells us that it was a faying among the pilgrims, that he was clean of deadly fin that could creep under that ftone. Bunfen denies that the ancient fupports were really lions. *Befchreibung*, ii. 157.

[1] *Caefar, tantus eras quantus et orbis:*
Sed nunc in medico clauderis antro.

Thefe verfes are the commencement of an epitaph

And this memorial was confecrated after their fafhion, as ftill appeareth, and may be read thereon. [And below in Greek letters thefe verfes be written:

> If one, tell how this ftone was fet on high;
> If many ftones, fhow where their joints do lie.][2]

2. *Of the Bafin, and the Golden Pine-cone, in Saint Peter's Parvife.*

IN Saint Peter's Parvife is a Bafin,[3] that was made by Pope Symmachus,[4]

---

or poem referred by William of Malmefbury to the emperor Henry III. (d. 1056). *De Gestis regum Anglorum*, l. ii. c. 12; Jordan, *Topographie*, ii. 373; Graf, i. 296.

[2] *Si lapis eft unus, dic qua fit arte levatus;*
    Et fi fint plures, dic ubi contigui.

This epigram is added in a manufcript of the fourteenth century. The Latin lines may have been written in Greek letters to excite curiofity.

[3] *In Paradifo fancti Petri eft cantarum.* The Paradife, or Parvife, of St. Peter was the Atrium in front of the Bafilica.

[4] So Anaftafius in the life of Symmachus: *Cantharum beati Petri cum quadriportieu marmoribus ornavit, et ex mufivo fecit agnos et cruces et palmas. Ipfum vero atrium marmoribus compaginavit: gradus vero ante fores bafilicae b. Petri ampliavit. Lib. Pont.*

and dight with pillars of porphyry, that are joined together by marble tables with griffons, and covered with a coftly fky of brafs,[5] with flowers, and dolphins of brafs gilt, pouring forth water. In the midft of the bafin is a brazen Pine-cone, the which, with a roof[6] of gilded brafs, was the covering over the ftatue of Cybele, mother of the gods, in the opening of the Pantheon.[7] Into this Pine-cone water out of the Sabbatine Aqueduct was fupplied under ground by a pipe of lead; the which being always full, gave water through holes in the nuts to all that wanted it;[8] and by the pipe under ground some part thereof flowed to the emperor's bath near the Needle.

[5] *Pretiofo celo aereo coopertae.*
[6] *Cum finino* [*fimo* Monfaucon].
[7] See page 48; and note 153.
[8] The Pine-cone is now in the Giardino della Pigna at the Vatican. The fupply of water through the nuts is fpoken of as a thing of the paft; the Pigna does not, as far as I can fee, give evidence of having been fo ufed. But fee Lanciani, *Atti dell' Accad. dei Lincei*, x. 513.

3. *Of the Sepulchre of Romulus, and the Terebinth of Nero.*

IN the *Naumachia*[9] is the sepulchre of Romulus, that is called *Meta*, or the Goal;[140] which aforetime was incased

---

[9] The name *Naumachia* in this district first appears in the life of Leo III. (796-816), who founded a hospital *in loco qui Naumachia dicitur.* (*Lib. Pontif.*) The hospital was dedicated to S. Peregrinus, and its site is marked by the little church of S. Pellegrino near the Porta Angelica. But the name extended over a wide area. A *regio Naumachiæ* appears in the acts of St. Sebastian, and the Leonine city was popularly said to be *in Almachia* (Anon. Magliab. Urlichs, *Codex,* 149, 161). Possibly the site where the name first appears by S. Pellegrino, may indicate the position of one of the naval amphitheatres of imperial times.

[140] The pyramid, which in the fifth or sixth century was believed to be the sepulchre of Scipio Africanus (Acro, *Schol. ad Hor. Epod.* ix. 25), and in the twelfth was called *Meta* or *Sepulcrum Romuli*, was destroyed by Pope Alexander VI. according to a note inserted upon the great Mantuan plan, published by De Rossi (*Piante,* tav. vi-xii). It stood on part of the present site of the church and monastery of S. Maria Transpontina, the old church having been nearer to the mausoleum of Hadrian. Its position is well ascertained by the medieval plans

with marvellous ſtone, wherewith was made the pavement of the Parviſe and the ſteps of Saint Peter. It had about it an open court of twenty feet, paved with the ſtone that cometh from Tibur, with its drain and border of flowers.¹ About it was the Terebinth of Nero,² of

of Rome, and by the plan of Bufalini. Some remains of ancient *opus quadratum* of tufo, uſed in the repair of the wall of the corridor leading from the Vatican Palace to the Caſtle, cloſe to the Via della Porta del Caſtello, and which may be ſeen in the ſtonemaſon's yard there, are probably the reſult of the demolition of the pyramid; the outer caſing of marble or travertine had been before removed, as appears from the text. The corridor, which ſeems to have been formed upon the ancient wall by Innocent VII. and repaired by Alexander VI. is called in Bufalini's plan *ambulatorium Alexandri ſexti*. His arms, with the date 1492, are over the entrance to the quarters of the Swiſs Guard.

¹ *Habuit circa ſe plateam Tiburtinam viginti pedum cum cloaca et florali ſuo.* The pyramid in its diſmantled ſtate was called by the leſs learned pilgrims St. Peter's corn-heap (*acervus ſegatis S. Petri*), which was ſaid to have turned into a hill of ſtone when Nero took poſſeſſion of it. Higden, *Polychron.* ed. Babington, i. 230.

² *Circa ſe habuit terbentinum* [al. *terebinta*] *Neronis* The Terebinth (ἡ τερέβινθος) near the Naumachia is mentioned in ſome Greek Acts of SS. Peter and Paul.

no less height than the Castle of Hadrian, [that is called the Angel's Castle],³ incased with marvellous stone, from which the work of the steps and the Paradise was finished. This building was round like a castle with two circles, whereof the lips were covered with tables of stone for dripping. Nigh thereunto was Saint Peter the Apostle crucified.⁴

(*Acta Apochr.* ed Tischendorf, p. 37, cited by Jordan, *Topographie*, vol. ii. p. xvii.); and in an Order for the emperor's coronation, probably of the eleventh century, he is described as taking the oath to observe the rights of the Roman people at S. Maria Transpontina which is near the Terebinth. (Gregorovius, *Hist.* Ital. transl. iv. 70.) It is perhaps the same monument which in the ordo of Benedictus Canonicus is called *obeliscus Neronis*. (See *Ordo Romanus*, Extracts 1 and 4; and see note 144). It appears to have been destroyed in the twelfth century, as the *Mirabilia* records only an exaggerated tradition of its magnificence. The origin of its medieval name is obscure. The word denotes a turpentine-tree, and among the local objects in the bas-relief of St. Peter's Crucifixion, on the bronze door of St. Peter's, a tall tree between the mausoleum and the Pyramid appears to symbolize the Terebinth.

³ This addition is from a manuscript of the fourteenth century. See note 145.

⁴ This seems to agree with the ecclesiastical

4. *Of the Castle of Crescentius.*[5]

MOREOVER, there is a castle, that was the temple of Hadrian, as we read in the Sermon of the festival of Saint Peter, where it saith: The memorial of the emperor Hadrian, a temple built up, of marvellous greatness and beauty;[6] the which was all covered with stones and adorned with divers histories, and fenced with brazen railings round

---

tradition. See note 126. *Acta SS. Petri et Pauli. Supervenit autem populus infinitus ad locum qui appellatur Naumachia iuxta obeliscum Neronis. Illic enim crux posita est.* Mombritius, f. 199.

[5] The mausoleum of Hadrian, in the tenth century popularly called *domus Theodorici*, obtained the name of Castle of Crescentius after the obstinate defence of it by Crescentius against the emperor Otho III. in 998. Before the end of the twelfth century it was called the Castle of the Holy Angel. Gregorovius, *Hist.* Ital. transl. iii. 520, iv. 343.

[6] The sermon here mentioned, by an unknown author, follows the sermons of Leo the Great in manuscripts of that work. It contains nothing further about the monument here named. *Leonis Magni Opera*, Ven. 1753. *Appendix Sermonum*, n. xvi. f. 442.

about, with golden peacocks and a bull, of the which peacocks two were thofe that are at the Bafin of the Parvife.⁷ At the four fides of the temple were four horfes of gilded brafs, and in every face were brazen gates. In the midft of the circle was the porphyry fepulchre of Hadrian, that is now at the Lateran before the Fullery,⁸ and is the fepulchre of Pope Innocent; and the cover is in Saint Peter's Parvife upon the Prefect's tomb.⁹ Below were gates of brafs as they now appear. †And in the porphyry monument of the bleffed Helen is buried pope Anaftatius the Fourth.†¹⁵⁰

---

⁷ Two bronze peacocks are now in the Garden of the Pigna, at the Vatican.

⁸ *Ante folloniam*. See the third extract from the *Ordo Romanus* in the Mirabiliana. Pope Innocent II. died 24 Sept. 1143. Johannes Diaconus, who wrote under Alexander V. (1254-1261), places his borrowed farcophagus in the nave of the church. Mabillon, *Mus. Ital.* ii. 568.

⁹ The prefect was Cinthius, or Cencius, who died 1079. Gregorovius, *Hift.* Ital. tranfl. iv. 245.

¹⁵⁰ Anaftafius IV. died 3 Dec. 1154, and was buried in the Lateran Bafilica, in the farcophagus of Helena, which he had brought to Rome from

The monuments whereof we have spoken were dedicated for temples, and the Roman maidens flocked to them with vows, as Ovid faith in the book of *Fasti*.

5. *Of the Sepulchre of Augustus.*

AT the Flaminean Gate Octavian made a castle, that is called *Augustum*,[1] to be the burying-place of the emperors; which was incased in divers kinds of stone. Within there is an hollow, leading into the circle by hidden ways. In the lower circle are the sepultures of emperors, and in each sepulture

---

her church on the via Labicana. (Johan. Diaconus, Mabillon, *Mus. Ital.* ii. 169.) The sarcophagus is now in the Vatican Museum.

[1] The mausoleum of Augustus seems never to have lost the name of its great founder. The name *Augustum* is found in the eighth century, and continued to the twelfth. In the thirteenth it was called *Augusta*; and in the fifteenth century it was popularly known as *Lausta*. Gregorovius, *Hist.* Ital. transl. ii. 357, iii. 663, v. 245; *Anon. Magl.* Urlichs, *Codex*, 162.

are letters saying after this fashion: These be the bones and ashes of Nerva emperor, and such and such was the victory he won;[2] and before it stood the image of his god, as in all the other sepulchres. In the midst of the sepultures is a recess where Octavian was wont to sit; and the priests were there, doing their ceremonies. And from every kingdom of the whole world he commanded that there should be brought one basket full of earth, the which he put upon the temple, to be a remembrance unto all nations coming to Rome.

[2] The emperor Nerva was in fact buried in the Mausoleum of Augustus; and Jordan suspected that the writer had some knowledge of a base inscribed with his name, which may have been at that time dug out of the monument. The now well-known inscriptions, *Ossa Agrippinae M. Agrippae*, *Ossa C. Caesaris Augusti f. principis inventutis*, etc. derived from the same source, were not known to the earlier epigraphists (Jordan, *Topographie*, ii. 435). The base inscribed to Agrippina is now in the court of the Palace of the Conservators.

6. *Of divers places between the Sepulchre of Augustus and the Capitol.*

IN the top of the Pantheon, that is to say of the Round Saint Mary's, stood the golden pine-cone that is now before the door of Saint Peter;[3] and the church was all covered with tables of gilded brass, insomuch that from afar it seemed as it were a mountain of gold;[4] whereof the beauty is still discerned in part. And] in the top of the front of the Pantheon stood two bulls of gilded brass. Before the palace of Alexander[5] were

---

[3] See p. 74. The story of the Pigna having been upon the Pantheon probably arose from the name of the region (Rione della Pigna), in which the Pantheon was the principal building.

[4] This is a reminiscence of the tiles of gilded bronze, which were taken away by the Byzantine emperor, Constans II. in 663.

[5] The palace of Alexander is apparently the Alexandrine Thermæ. The imaginary temple of Flora and Phœbus and that of Bellona illustrate the propensity of the Mirabilian writer to convert all the ancient ruins into temples. Other examples occur in every subsequent page.

two temples, of Flora and Phœbus. Behind the palace, where the Shell now is, was the temple of Bellona. There was it written:

> Old Rome was I, now new Rome shall be praised;
> I bear my head aloft, from ruin raised.⁶

At the Shell of Parione was the temple of Gnaeus Pompeius of marvellous greatness and beauty; and his monument, that is called Majorent, was fairly adorned, and was an oracle of Apollo; and there were other oracles in other places.⁷

⁶ *Roma vetusta fui, sed nunc nova Roma vocabor:*
Eruta ruderibus culmen ad alta fero.

These lines are not known elsewhere. They seem to belong to the era of political revival in the middle of the twelfth century. (Gregorovius, *Hist.* Ital. Transl. iv. 518, 550.) The Shell (*concha*) where they are said to have been written was a Fountain or Basin.

⁷ The theatre of Pompey becomes his temple according to the system referred to in note 155. The *conca Parionis* was probably an antique basin in the region of Parione; before the beginning of the fourteenth century it had been removed to the hospital of St. James at the Colosseum. (*Anon. Magl.* Urlichs, *Codex*, 163). The majorent (*maioretum* al. *maiorentum*) was perhaps part of the

The church of Saint Urſus was Nero's Chancery.[8] In the Palace of Antoninus was the temple of Divus Antoninus.[9] By Saint Saviour,[10] before Saint Mary *in Aquiro*, the temple of Ælius Hadrianus, and the Arch of Pity.[1] In the Field of Mars[2] the temple of Mars, where conſuls were elected in the Calends of June, and they tarried till the Calends

buildings grouped with the theatre. A church of S. Maria *in majurente* occurs in the twelfth century. Cencius, in Mabillon, *Mus. Ital.* ii. 195.

[8] *Secretarium Neronis.* If the church of St. Urſus is that near the Bridge of S. Angelo (ſee p. 10), the pilgrim makes a freſh ſtart here.

[9] The Palace of Antoninus was the ruins near the Antonine column. So in chapter 8, *columna Antonini in palatio ſuo*.

[10] The words *iuxta Sanctum Salvatorem* may belong either to the preceding or to the following clauſe. The church is not known: S. Salvatore della Coppelle was founded 1195, later than the Mirabilia. Martinelli, *Roma Sacra*, 398.

[1] See p. 14. Lanciani places the arch of Pity or Piety in an open place, oppoſite the Porticus of the Pantheon. *Atti dei Lincei*, Ser. III. ix. 387.

[2] *In Campo Martio* The Campus Martius of the 12th century was a reſtricted ſpace, poſſibly at the Piazza now ſo named, where ſome ancient remains are built up in a houſe on the weſt ſide.

of January; and if he that was chosen
conful was clear of crime, his confulſhip
was confirmed to him. [And by reaſon
of this cuſtom many be yet called Confuls of the Romans.]³ In this temple
did the Roman conquerors ſet the beaks
of their enemies' ſhips, whereof were
made works to be a ſight for all nations.
Nigh unto the Pantheon was the temple
of Minerva Chalcidica, [where ſome
pillars of marble are ſtill ſeen].⁴ Behind Saint Mark's, the temple of Apollo.
In the Camillanum, where is Saint

³ This is a curious alluſion to the uſe of the
title *Conful* by the chief magiſtrates of Rome in the
eleventh and twelfth centuries. See Gregorovius,
Hiſt. Ital. tranſl. iv. 20, 430.

⁴ This addition is from Montfaucon's text,
probably of the fourteenth century. In a map of
the fifteenth century ſome ruins are ſhown adjoining
the church of S. Maria ſopra Minerva to the eaſt.
De Roſſi, *Piante*, tav. iv. The ſmall obeliſk which
is now before the Pantheon, and was formerly,
until 1711, in the little ſquare before S. Macuto,
is not alluded to in the text. We may perhaps
conclude that it was excavated at a later time. It
is ſhown in a map of about 1475, when it had
already acquired the legendary name of Sepulchre
of Brutus. See the map at the end of this volume.

Cyriac, was the temple of Vesta;[5] in the lime-kiln,[6] the temple of Venus; in the lady Rose's monastery, the Golden Castle, that was the oracle of Juno.[7]

7. *Of the Capitol.*[8]

THE Capitol [is so called, because it] was the head of the world, where the consuls and senators abode to govern the Earth. The face thereof was

---

[5] See p. 21, note 40.

[6] *In Calcarari.* S. Nicola ai Cesarini was called in the twelfth century *S. Nicolai Calcariorum (Ordo Cencii* in Mabillon, *Mus. Ital.* ii. 194). Lucius Faunus calls it S. Nicola in Calcaria (*Roma Ant.* f. 143). The ruins behind this church, now called the temple of Hercules Custos, may be the Mirabilian Temple of Venus.

[7] The *castellum aureum* was the Circus Flaminius; and the *monasterium dominae Rosae* is now S. Caterina ai Funari. Martinelli, *Roma Sacra*, 87.

[8] The north-eastern end of the Capitol was occupied in the twelfth century by the Tabularium, restored about 1143 as the Senators' Palace, and by the Abbey of St. Mary, to which in the beginning of the century the whole hill, ' with its stones, walls and columns,' had belonged. See the Bull of Anacletus II. among the Mirabiliana. The re-

covered with high walls and ftrong, rifing above the top of the hill, and covered all over with glafs and gold and marvellous carved work. †And in the Capitol were molten images of all the Trojan kings and of the emperors.†[9] Within the fortrefs was a palace all adorned with marvellous works in gold and filver and brafs and coftly ftones, to be a mirror to all nations; [the which was faid to be worth the third part of the world]. Moreover the temples that were within the fortrefs, and which

---

mainder of the hill appears to have become a rough garden or pafture, ftudded with ruins, for moft of which imaginary names were provided. Yet fuch was the power of its old affociations, that the Capitol was regarded as one of the 'feven wonders of the world.' During the three following centuries, the ruins were doubtlefs ufed to fupply materials for the new conftructions of the Palace and Monaftery. Poggio gives a defcription of the defolate condition of the hill about 1450. Poggius, *De Varietate Fortunae*, 5 ; Urlichs, *Codex*, 235.

[9] This appears to be a reminifcence of the ftatues of the kings mentioned by Appian, *Bell. Civ.* i. 16; Dio, xliii. 45; Pliny, xxiv. 5, 11; Suetonius, *Julius*, 76.

they can bring to remembrance,[170] be these. In the uppermost part of the fortress,[1] over the *Porticus Crinorum*, was the temple of Jupiter and Moneta, as is found in Ovid's Martyrology of the *Fasti*, †wherein was Jupiter's image of gold, sitting on a throne of gold.† Towards the market-place,[2] the temple

---

[170] *Quae infra arcem fuere quae ad memoriam ducere possunt.* Urlichs prints *possum* without remark.

[1] *In summitate arcis.* The *Porticus Crinorum*, or part of it, was between St. Nicholas in carcere and the Capitol (*Ordo Romanus*, Extract 1, in Mirabiliana.) High above on this side of the hill appear to have been the remains of the south corner of the Capitoline temple of Jupiter (*Templum maius quod respicit super Alaphantum*. Bull of Anaclete II. Translated in Mirabiliana). Poggio describes himself as sitting in the ruins of the Tarpeian fortress behind what seemed the huge threshold of the door of a temple with broken columns about, the spot being one which commanded a view of the greatest part of the city. (Poggius, *De Var. Fort.* 5.) It is probably these ruins which are shown in the plan copied at the end of this volume. The name of Moneta was no doubt supplied by the 'Martyrology' of Ovid. *Fasti*, vi. 183.

[2] *In partem fori.* The ancient Roman Forum seems out of the question, as it had ceased to be a

of Vesta and Cæsar; there was the chair of the pagan pontiffs, wherein the senators did set Julius Cæsar on the sixth day of the month of March.[3] On the other side of the Capitol, over *Cannapara*,[4] the temple of Juno. Fast by the public market-place[5] the temple of Hercules.

---

public place, and there is no sign of its locality being remembered. See chapter 10, note 195. Jordan suggests the Piazza del Campidoglio as a fit place for the enthronement of Cæsar. (*Topographie*, ii. 462.) The Piazza di Ara Celi was a market-place in the twelfth century. See the Bull of Anacletus II. among the Mirabiliana.

[3] The sixth day of March was marked in the ancient calendar as the day on which Cæsar Augustus assumed the pontificate. (Foggoni, *Fasti*, pp. 23, 107; *Corp. Inscr. Lat.* i. 314). The occasion is mentioned by Ovid (*Fasti*, iii. 419),

Caesaris innumeris, quem maluit ille mereri,
    Accessit titulis pontificalis honos.

It was a natural mistake to assume that Julius was meant.

[4] In the direction of the Basilica Julia; See chapter 10.

[5] It is not clear whether the *forum publicum* is the same as the *forum* already named. Bunsen suggests the Piazza del Campidoglio. *Beschreibung*, iii. 2, 128.

In the Tarpeian hill,[6] the temple of *Afilis*, where Julius Cæsar was flain of the Senate.[7] In the place where Saint Mary's now ftandeth were two temples together, joined with a palace, to wit, the temples of Phœbus and of Carmentis, where the emperor Octavian faw the vifion in heaven.[8] Faft by the Camellaria was the temple of Janus, that was the warden of the Capitol.[9] And it was therefore called Golden Capitol, becaufe it excelled in wifdom and beauty before all the realms of the whole world.

[6] It is quite uncertain, whether any fpecial part of the Capitol was known as the Tarpeian Hill in the Mirabilian time.

[7] So Shakfpeare: "I did enact Julius Cæfar; I was killed i' the Capitol." (*Hamlet*, act iii. fcene 2.) A remote example of the influence of Mirabilian legend.

[8] See p. 35.

[9] The Camellaria appears to have been in the ruins of the temple of Concord. See the Bull of Anacletus II. among the Mirabiliana. The 'temple of Janus' may have been that of Vefpafian, or poffibly a ruin below the church of Ara Celi, towards the Prifon. Janus, as *cuftos Capitolii*, is a reminifcence of Ovid. *Fafti*, i. 259-272.

8. *Of the Palace of Trajan and his Forum, and of the Temples nigh thereunto.*

THE palace of Trajan and Hadrian was built well nigh all of stones,[180] and adorned throughout with marvellous works, and ceiled with many diverse colours; where is a pillar of marvellous highness and beauty, with graven work of the stories of these emperors, in like fashion as the pillar of Antonine in his palace; and on the one side was the temple of *Divus Traianus*, and on the other, of *Divus Hadrianus*.[1]

In the Silversmith's Hill[2] was the

---

[180] *Pene totum lapidibus constructum.* Probably marbles are meant.

[1] Perhaps the remains of the Basilica Ulpia, and of the temple of Trajan.

[2] *In clivo argentarii.* The temples of Concord, Saturn, Vespasian, and Titus are from the Notitia, where they follow in the same order the Basilica Argentaria. But Concord and Saturn are here paired together in one temple, instead of Vespasian and Titus. Some of these temples reappear in the next chapter.

temple of Concord and Saturn. In *Tofula* the temple of Bacchus.³ In the end of the *Infula Argentaria* the temple of Vespasian. In the hill of Saint Mary *in campo* the temple of Titus.⁴ Where Saint Basil standeth, was the temple of Carmentis.⁵ Within these bounds⁶ was a Palace with two

---

³ A church of S. Maria *in Tofella* is mentioned by Cencius (Mabillon, *Mus. Ital.* ii. 192). The site is uncertain.

⁴ The church of *S. Maria in Campo* is placed in Bufalini's plan on the slope of the Quirinal hill, a little south of S. Agata. But the church of *S. Maria in Campo Carleone* existed until a few years ago at the western end on the south side of the existing Via Campo Carleone. See Nolli's plan, dated 1748.

⁵ St. Basil, an ancient monastery built in the ruins of the temple of Mars Ultor in the Forum of Augustus, is now the convent of the Nuns of the S. Annunziata.

⁶ *Infra hunc terminum.* The monastery of St. Basil was partly inclosed by the lofty wall of the Forum of Augustus, which was continued to the south by that of the Forum of Nerva. The former forum had lost its name, and the name of Trajan was extended over a wider area. So Petrus Mallius, *Ecclesia S. Basilii iuxta palatium Traiani imperatoris.* (Mabillon, *Mus. Ital.* ii. 161.) The

Forums, the Forum of Nerva with his temple of *Divus Nerva*, and the greater Forum of Trajan; before the gate whereof was the temple of *Sospita Dea*. Where Saint Quiricus is, was the temple of Jupiter.[7]

In the wall of Saint Basil was fixed a great table of brass, where in a good and notable place was written the league that was between the Romans and Jews in the time of Judas Maccabeus.[8]

---

remains of the temple of Minerva, dedicated by Nerva, and here called the temple of Nerva (being identified by its inscription), were destroyed by Pope Paul V.

[7] The gate of the forum of Trajan may be the Porta dei Pantani, which however appears to have been closed. See *Ordo Romanus*, Extract 2, in Mirabiliana. St. Quiricus still exists in the Via Tor dei Conti.

[8] Maccabees, viii. 22. Jordan suggests, that the story of the bronze tablet, which the writer does not seem to have seen, may have arisen from an inscription formerly existing by the church of St. Basil. *C. Iulius Caesar Strabo aed. cur . . . . iud. pontif. Corpus Inscr. Lat.* i. 278; Jordan, *Topographie*, ii. 470.

9. *Of the Temple of Mars by the Prison of Mamertinus, and of other buildings nigh unto Saint Sergius his Church.*

BEFORE Mamertinus his prison was the temple of Mars, where is now his image.[9] Nigh unto him was the Fatal Temple, that is, Saint Martina; nigh whereunto is the temple of Refuge, that is, Saint Hadrian. Fast by is another Fatal Temple.[190] Nigh unto

---

[9] The statue called Marforio, removed in the sixteenth century to the Piazza del Campidoglio, and to the Court of the Capitoline Museum in or about 1668. *Roma Antica e Moderna*, ed. 1668, p. 661.

[190] The Fatal Temple was suggested by the name, *in Tribus Fatis*, given to the site of the church of S. Martina, probably from the Sibyls' statues, called the Three Fates. (Procopius, *Bell. Goth.* i. 25; *Lib. Pontif.* Leo III. § 413). If there is no misreading, the second Fatal Temple may have been the ruin described by Labacco and others, and thought by some archæologists to be the Janus of Domitian, and by others part of the Æmilian Basilica. Labacco, *Architettura*, tav. 17; Lanciani, *Atti dei Lincei*, Ser. III. vol. xi. p. 1; Hülsen, *Annali dell' Inst.* 1884, p. 323.

the public prifon, the temple of the Fabii.[1] Behind Saint Sergius, the temple of Concord, before which is the Triumphal Arch, whence was the afcent into the Capitol by the public Treafury,[2] that was the temple of Saturn. On the other fide was an arch encafed with marvellous ftones, whereon was the ftory how the foldiers received their gifts from the Senate through the Treafurer,[3] that had the charge of this bufinefs, all the which gifts he weighed in a Balance, before they were given to the foldiers; whence it is called Saint

---

[1] The Fabian Arch probably ftood at the weft corner of the temple of Fauftina. See note 200. But the name of Fabius appears to have migrated to the neighbourhood of the Prifon.

[2] *Iuxta acrarium publicum.* The fituation of the temples of Concord and Saturn (the *aerarium*) and of the *clivus Capitolinus* appears to have been rightly known. The church of St. Sergius, removed between 1539 and 1551, ftood on the fouth corner of the ruins of Concord. (Nichols, *Notizie dei Roftri*, 65-71.) The ancient afcent is fpoken of in the paft tenfe.

[3] *Per faccellarium.*

Saviour *de Statera*, that is to say, of the Balance.[4]

10. *Of Cannapara, and the place called Hell; and of the Temples between Cannapara and the Arch of Seven Lamps.*[5]

IN *Cannapara* is the temple of Ceres and Tellus, with two courts or houses, adorned all around with porches resting upon pillars, so that whosoever sat therein for to give judgment was

---

[4] It is impossible to say what foundation there may have been for this story of an arch, which, it should be observed, is not spoken of as existing. Perhaps the whole was suggested by the additional name of the church, the origin of which name is unknown. The church seems to have been on the south side of the Capitol (Jordan, *Topographie*, ii. 483-487), possibly the church now called S. Omobuono, formerly S. Salvatore *in porticu*. Martinelli, *Roma Sacra*, 291.

[5] In this chapter the visitor is led from the south side of the Capitol, across the Roman Forum, and up the Sacred way; but it should be observed, that the names of these famous localities appear to have been forgotten.

seen from every side.⁶ Fast by that house was the palace of Catiline, where was a church of Saint Antony;⁷ nigh whereunto is a place that is called Hell, because of old time it burst forth there;⁸ and brought great mischief upon Rome; where a certain noble knight,

⁶ There can be little doubt, both from the situation and description of the ruin, that the Cannapara was the Basilica Julia, the remains of which were in a garden belonging to the hospital of Our Lady of Consolation, and were used for a long period of time as a quarry, as is evidenced by the leases or licenses granted for that purpose, preserved among the records of the hospital. The basilica, which was principally used as a law-court, was erroneously identified with the temple of Tellus, attributed by ecclesiastical tradition to the same use. See note 69.

⁷ The palace of Catiline was probably the ruin of the temple of Castor. Suetonius mentions Catiline's house in the Palatine (*De Grammaticis*, 17). Nothing is known of the church of St. Antony, which appears to have disappeared before the description was written. In the lower part of the great ruin behind the temple some religious paintings were found a few years since.

⁸ *Locus qui dicitur infernus, eo quod antiquo tempore ibi eructuabat.* This name is still preserved in that of the church of S. Maria *Libera nos a poenis Inferni*. The hollow vaults under the towering ruins of the

to the intent that the city fhould be delivered after the refponfes of their gods, did on his harnefs and caft himfelf into the pit, and the earth clofed; fo the city was delivered. There is the temple of Vefta,[9] where it is faid that a dragon coucheth below, as we read in the life of Saint Silvefter.[200]

The temple of Pallas is there, and

Palatine feem to have fuggefted fearful affociations, which recalled at the fame time the yawning pit of Curtius and the legendary cave of St. Silvefter.

[9] There is reason to believe, that confiderable remains of the temple of Vefta exifted above ground in the twelfth century. See Lanciani, *Atti dei Lincei*, Ser. III. vol. x. p. 349.

[200] The legend of St. Silvefter and the dragon was affociated with various localities in Rome. The ancient legendaries place it in the Capitol, the *Ordo Romanus* of Benedict near St. Lucia in Orpheo. (See Extract 6, in Mirabiliana.) Among the pilgrims the *Infernus*, by the temple of Vefta, was believed to be the fpot. (See Church Marvels, c. 13, in Mirabiliana.) In the later medieval legendary no fpecial locality is mentioned, but the faint defcends into the pit by an hundred and fifty-two fteps, binds the mouth of the dragon, and fhuts him in there until the day of doom. Pet. de Natalibus, *Acta S. Silvefiri*, f. 22.

Cæsar's Forum,[1] and the temple of Janus, who forseeth the year in his beginning and in his end, as Ovid faith in the *Fasti;* now is it called Cencio Frangipane's Tower.[2] The temple of

---

[1] From the temple of Vesta the visitor is conducted northward to the other side of the Roman Forum. The first building passed in this direction would include the marble walls of the Regia, perhaps the 'temple of Pallas' of the text. The 'temple of Pallas' before the portico of Faustina is said to have been demolished under Paul III. (Magnan, *Città di Roma,* i. 34.) This was the time of the removal of the remains of the Regia. Further north was the Mirabilian Forum of Cæsar, which lay to the right of the road leading from St. Hadrian to the temple of Minerva in the Forum of Nerva. *Ordo Romanus,* Extract 4.

[2] Cencio Frangipane was a leader of one of the Roman factions in the first half of the twelfth century. The fortresses of this family, which included the arch of Titus, appear also to have extended across the bottom of the Sacra Via. The tower, built on a ruin here called the temple of Janus, was perhaps upon a part of the temple of Julius. It was united, with an ancient arch, to the church of St. Laurence, that is, to the temple of Faustina. A massive arch of masonry which existed till the middle of the sixteenth century near the west corner of this temple, and is shewn in

Minerva with an arch is joined thereunto, but it is now called Saint Laurence *de Mirandi*. Faſt by is the church of Saint Coſmas, that was the temple of Aſylum. Behind was the temple of Peace and Latona, and above the ſame, the temple of Romulus.[3] Behind New Saint Mary, two temples of Concord and Piety.[4] Nigh unto the arch of Seven Lamps the temple of Æſculapius;

ſeveral early drawings, has been conjectured to be the arch here mentioned, and poſſibly the remains of the arch of Fabius. See the Proceedings of the Roman Archæological Inſtitute of this year, 1888.

[3] The name of *Aſylum*, given to the round church, was perhaps ſuggeſted by that of Romulus, which was its original deſignation but had paſſed to the adjoining baſilica. The ancient building behind, on the walls of which the marble plan of Rome, partly preſerved in the Capitoline Muſeum, was hung, appears to have adjoined the Forum of Peace. The Baſilica of Conſtantine, to which the name of temple of Peace was afterwards transferred, was called the temple (or palace) of Romulus. See p. 20. The name of Latona was derived from the learned name of an adjoining arch, popularly called Arco del Latrone. See *Ordo Romanus*, Extract 6; *Anon Magl.* Urlichs, *Codex*, 106.

[4] See p. 20.

it is therefore called Cartulary, becaufe there was a common library there,[5] of which there were twenty and eight in the city.[6]

11. *Of the Palatine Hill, and the parts nigh thereunto.*

ABOVE the arch of Seven Lamps was the temple of Pallas,[7] and

---

[5] The arch of Seven Lamps and the Cartulary Tower have been mentioned, p. 11. There is fome evidence of an ancient temple of Æfculapius near the Coloffeum (Jordan, *Topographie*, ii. 508). The Cartulary Tower was fo called from having been a Papal Archive in connection with a palace exifting on this fide of the Palatine in the eighth and ninth centuries. (De Roffi, *Bull. del Inft.* 1884, p. 5.) It was afterwards part of the Frangipane fortrefs, and was deftroyed in 1237.

[6] This is from the Notitia. Urlichs, *Codex*, 21.

[7] The monaftery of St. Sebaftian, alfo called S. Maria in Pallara, ftill exifting on the Palatine near the Arch of Titus, appears to have derived its name from an ancient *palladium palatinum* mentioned in an infcription of the time of Conftantine. (De Roffi, *Bull. di Archæol. Crift.* 1867, p. 15.) In a former page (p. 16) the Palatine Hill is called *Pallanteum*, in allufion to Virgil, *Aen.* viii 53.

*Delegere locum, et pofuere in montibus urbem
Pallantis proavi de nomine Pallanteum.*

the temple of Juno. Within Palatium
is the temple of Julian; in the front of
Palatium, the temple of the Sun; in
the same Palatium, the temple of
Jupiter, that is called *Casa maior*.
Where Saint Cæsarius is, was the Augu-
ratory of Cæsar.*

Before the Colosseum was the temple
of the Sun, where ceremonies were done
to the image that stood on the top of
the Colosseum, †having on his head a
crown of gold dight with gems, whose
head and hand are now before the
Lateran.†⁹ The Septizonium was the
temple of the Sun and Moon, before
which was the temple of Fortune.
Saint Balbina † in Albiston † was the
shifting-place of Cæsar. †There was a
candlestick made of the stone *Albiston*,

---

* The temple of Julian is unknown. The
temple of the Sun is probably the same as that
below. The *Casa major* was the group of imperial
palaces. S. Cæsarius may have been a church of
that name in the Palatine, and not the well-known
church on the Via Appia. The *Auguratcrium* (not
Cæsaris) occurs in the Notitia, Region X. *Palatium.*

⁹ See pp. 62, 64.

which, once kindled and fet in the open air, was **never by any** means quenched. There, moreover, **is** the image **of our** Lord behind the altar, painted by no human **hand, after** the fafhion wherein our Lord **was in the flefh. The** which place **is therefore** called *Albefta* becaufe the *albae ftolae*, that is **to** fay the white ftoles, **of the emperors were there made.†** There were the **Severian and** Commodian **Thermæ. Where Saint** Sabba is, was the Area **of Apollo and of Spleen.**[210]

12. *Of the Circus of Tarquin.*

THE circus of Prifcus Tarquinius was of marvellous beauty: the which was in fuch wife built up with degrees, that no Roman hindered an-

---

[210] *Mutatorium Caefaris, Thermae Severianae et Commodianae, Area Apollinis et Splenis* are all from the Notitia, Region I. *Porta Capena.* The localities are probably arbitrary. The meaning of the name *Albifton* is unknown. Two fanciful derivations are fuggefted in the text. See p. 32.

other in the feeing of the games.¹ At the top were arches all around, ceiled with glafs and fhining gold. Around, were the houfes of the Palace above, where the women fat to fee the games on the fourteenth day of the Calends of May, when the games were held.² In the midft were two Needles;³ the leffer had eighty and feven feet of height, but the greater one hundred twenty and two. On the top of the triumphal arch, that is at the head of the Circus, ftood a horfeman of gilded brafs, which feemed to prefs forward, as though the

---

¹ The Circus Maximus is learnedly introduced, not by its popular name of *Stadium* (fee p. 31, note 70), but as the Circus of Prifcus Tarquinius (Liv. i. 35). The form of the feats alluded to above is fhewn in the drawings of the fixteenth century.

² The thirteenth of the kalends of May was marked in the calendar as the laft day of the *ludi Cereri in Circo*, which continued eight days. *Corp. Infcr. Lat.* i. 305, 391.

³ *Duae aguliae:* two obelifks, the greater of which (fomewhat fhortened at the bafe) is now at the Lateran, and the leffer in the Piazza del Popolo. The heights are from the Region Book. Urlichs, *Codex*, 21.

rider would have the horse to run. On another arch, that is at the end,[4] stood another horseman of gilded brass in like fashion. †These images with all their harness made of brass were carried away by the emperor Constantine to Constantinople, Damascus and Alexandria.†[5] In the height of the Palace were chairs for the emperor and the queen, from which they were wont to see the games.

[4] *In alio arcu qui est in fine.* These descriptions seem to imply that two arches were standing in the twelfth century. One only is mentioned at p. 10, *in circo arcus Titi et Vespasiani*, unless *arcus* be here treated as plural. The arch at the round end belonged in the tenth century to the monastery of St. Gregory, and was demised in 1145 to the Frangipani. Mittarelli, *Ann. Cam.* 1 App. 96, 3 App. 417, cited by Jordan, *Topographie*, ii. 514.

[5] Constantine added to the ornament of the Circus, and his son Constantius erected the greater obelisk. The text is founded on a mistaken reminiscence of the plunder of Roman monuments by Constans II. in 663, when the bronze roof of the Pantheon was removed.

13. *From the Cælian Hill to Saint Crofs in Jerufalem.*

IN the Cælian hill was Scipio's temple. Before the Maximian Thermæ were two fhells,[6] and two temples of Ifis and Serapis. In the Orphan-houfe[7] the temple of Apollo. In the palace of Lateran are things to be marvelled at, but not to be written.[8] In the Sufurrian Palace was the temple of Hercules.[9]

[6] *Due concae* [al. *duo carceres*]. The Maximian Thermæ occur in the lift of thermæ, Part i. c. 6; but nothing is known about them, or the ruin here called Scipio's Temple, unlefs it be S. Stefano Rotondo.

[7] *In orphanotrophio.* A church of *S. Stephani orphanotrophii,* alfo called *in fchola cantorum,* is mentioned in old documents. Cencius, in Mabillon, *Mus. Ital.* ii. 194; Zaccagni, Mai. *Spicileg. Roman.* ix. 462.

[8] See p. 65, and further on, Church Marvels, chapter 4.

[9] See p. 20, note 36.

14. *Of the Eastern Quarter of the City.*

IN the Esquiline Hill[220] was the temple of Marius, that is now called *Cimbrum*, becauſe he conquered the Cimbrians, [where ſome pillars and images do yet appear].[1] In Licinius his palace, the temple of Honour and Diana.[2] Where Saint Mary the Greater

---

[220] The ſingular name for the Eſquiline, alluded to in the chapter on the Hills, p. 17, *Exquilinus qui ſupra* [al. *ſuper*] *alios dicitur*, is mentioned in Peter de Natalibus: *Hic edificavit ecclesiam Sanctae Dei Genitricis, quae dicitur ad Praeſepe et hodie Major vocatur, in monte Superagio iuxta macellum Libyae. Acta S. Sixti III.* See alſo Adinolfi, *Roma*, ii. 147.

[1] The images, commonly called the Trophies of Marius, were removed in 1585 to the parapet of the Piazza del Campidoglio.

[2] The Licinian Palace appears to have been in the Region called in the middle ages *Caput Tauri* (that is near the Gate of S. Lorenzo, ſee p. 7); and the temple of Honor and Diana is thought to be ſuggeſted by ſome knowledge of an *aedes Honoris et Virtutis*, founded by Caius Marius. Vitruvius, lib. vii. *praef.* Cicero, *Orat. pro Seſt.* 54, 56; *Corpus Inſcr. Lat.* i. 290. Jordan, *Topographie*, ii. 319, 518.

is, was the temple of Cybele. Where Saint Peter *ad vincula*, was the temple of Venus. At Saint Mary *in Fontana*, the temple of Faunus ; this was the idol that fpake to Julian, and beguiled him.³

In the palace of Diocletian were four temples, of Afclepius and Saturn and Mars and Apollo, the which are now called the Bufhels.⁴

At the head of the Three-Crofs-Ways⁵ was the temple of Venus, where

---

³ The temples of Cybele, Venus, and Faunus are without any known foundation. A church of S. Maria *in Fonticana* is mentioned (*Lib. Pont.* Leo III. § 362). The legend, that Julian was led aftray by the fpeech of an idol in the temple of Faunus, is not found elfewhere. There is another legend, that he took an idol of Mercury out of the Tiber, and the demon within it induced him to renounce Chriftianity, and gave him the empire. *Kaiferchronik*, cited by Graf, *Roma nel Medio Evo*, ii. 136.

⁴ *Nunc vocantur modii.* The round form of parts of the ruin of the Baths of Diocletian no doubt fuggefted this name. One of the Bufhels is now the church of S. Bernardo alle Terme.

⁵ *In capite trivii.* Whether the name *trivium* (the modern Trevi) is of claffical origin, is not certain. *Hortus Veneris* occurs in a Papal Bull,

it is yet called Venus' Garden. In the palace of Tiberius, the temple of the Gods.[6]

On the brow of the hill was the temple of Jupiter and Diana, that is now called the Emperor's Table, over the Palace of Conftantine.[7] There in the palace was the temple of Saturn and Bacchus, where their idols now lie. Faft by are the Marble Horfes.[8]

In the Thermæ of Olympias, where

relating to the boundaries of the parifh of SS. Apoftoli, attributed to John III. but probably of the twelfth century. Jordan, *Topographie*, ii. 526, 669. Urlichs, *Codex*, 200.

[6] *Templum deorum:* the names perhaps omitted by overfight. This palace of Tiberius feems from the order in which it is named to have been on the Quirinal.

[7] The ruin called *menfa imperatoris*, and later Frontifpizio di Nerone, is known by many drawings and engravings. It appears to have been deftroyed partly at the end of the feventeenth century and partly in 1722.

[8] The palace of Conftantine was the Conftantinian Thermæ, the ruins of which were oppofite the church of S. Silveftro a Monte Cavallo. The ftatues called Saturn and Bacchus were the two river-gods, now in the Piazza del Campidoglio.

Saint Laurence was broiled, was the temple of Apollo.⁹ Before the palace of Trajan, where the gate of the Palace yet remains, was a temple.²³⁰

15. *Of the parts of the City nigh unto the Tiber.*

IN the Aventine was the temple of Mercury looking towards the Circus; and the temple of Pallas; and Mercury's Well, where the merchants received refponses.¹ At the Arch of the Racecourfe, the houfe of Aurelia

---

⁹ See p. 18. The temple appears to be imaginary.

²³⁰ See p. 93, note 187.

¹ A temple of Minerva appears in fact to have been on this fide of the Aventine (Jordan, *Topographie*, ii. 530); and a *balneum Mercurii* is mentioned in the Einfiedeln Itinerary as on the Aventine above St. Mary in Cofmedin. The writer had probably Ovid in his mind (*Fafti*, v. 669).

> *Templa tibi pofuere patres fpectantia circum*
> *Idibus: ex quo eft haec tibi fefta dies.*
> *Te, quicunque fuas profitetur vendere merces*
> *Thure dato, tribuas ut fibi lucra, rogat.*

Auriftilla;[2] on one fide the temple of Mæcenas, and on the other fide the temple of Jupiter.

Nigh unto the Greek School was the palace of Lentulus.[3] On the other fide where now is the tower of Cencius de Orrigo, was the temple of Bacchus.[4]

At the gratings[5] was the temple of the Sun. The Round Saint Stephen

---

[2] Aurelia Oreftilla, wife of Catiline (Salluft. *Catilin. Coniur.* c. 15, 35.) The names of Lentulus and Catiline (p. 97) fuggefted this third name. The arch of the Circus has been mentioned, pp. 10, 104.

[3] This title of Palace of Lentulus is derived from an infcription (*P. Lentulus Cn. f. Scipio*, etc.) formerly upon an arch near the church of St. Mary in Cofmedin, or *in Schola Graeca*. Urlichs, *Codex*, 226.

[4] Cencio de Orrigo is not otherwife known. His tower may have been the building on the *Janus Quadrifrons*, of which the remains appear in Piranefi's engraving, and other views until the beginning of this century. But the *Velum Aureum* occurs later, p. 113.

[5] *Ad gradellas.* Jordan fuggefts, that the church of S. Maria Egiziaca was the fame as S. Maria *de Gradellis* (Cencius, in Mabillon, *Mus. Ital.* ii. 192). The fluted half-columns may have fuggefted the name; but there was alfo a church S. *Gregorii de Gradellis.* Jordan, *Topographie*, ii. 531, 534; Urlichs, *Codex*, 173; and fee note 356 in this volume.

was the temple of Faunus.[6] At the Elephant[7] the temple of the Sibyl; and the temple of Cicero at the Tullianum, †where now is the house of Peter Leone's sons. There is the *Carcer Tullianus*, that is to say, the Tullian prison, where is the church of Saint Nicolas. There night is the temple of Jupiter, where was the Golden Bower;[8] and the Severian temple, where Saint Angel is. At *Velum*

[6] The Round S. Stephen of the twelfth century was S. Stefano alle Carrozze in the Piazza Bocca di Verità, commonly known as the Temple of Vesta.

[7] *In Alephanto.* See note 171. Probably the *elefantus herbarius* of the Eighth Region (*Notitia.* Urlichs, *Codex*, 12). Elephantus also occurs in the Einsiedeln Itinerary, apparently between the theatre of Marcellus and the *Schola Graecorum*, i.e. St. Mary in Cosmedin (Urlichs, *Codex*, 68; Jordan, *Topographie*, ii. 657). In the map copied at the end of this volume, the name, *templum Sibyllae*, is given to that church.

[8] The original text, without the addition from the Graphia, runs as follows: *et templum Ciceronis in Tulliano est* [al. *et*] *templum Iovis ubi fuit pergula aurea.* The church of S. Niccolò *in carcere*, which stands on the site of three ancient temples, ac-

Aureum, that is to say, the Golden Vail,⁹ the temple of Minerva. At the Jews' Bridge the temple of Faunus ;²¹⁰ at Caccavari the temple of Craticula.¹

quired by an erroneous association of names the title, *in carcere Tulliano*. From this it was an easy step to Cicero. Pierleone, father of Pope Anaclete II. died 1128. His house under the Capitol (*qua Capitolii rupes aedibus Petri Leonis imminet, Vita Paschalis II.*) was near St. Nicolas, and probably included the ruins of the theatre of Marcellus. The temple of Jupiter appears to have been that of Jupiter Stator at the Porticus of Octavia, here called, from the inscription, the Severian Temple. Pergola d'oro may have been a popular name. The church of S. Angelo in Pescheria is called in a letter of the twelfth century *S. Angeli iuxta templam Jovis*. Gregorovius, *History*, Ital. transl. iv. 344, 424, 542; Mirabiliana, *Ordo Romanus*, Extract 1.

⁹ *Ad velum aureum*. The ancient *Velabrum*. See note 66.

²⁴⁰ *Idibus agrestis fumant altaria Fauni,*
Hic ubi discretas insula rumpit aquas.

Ovid, *Fasti*, ii. 193.

¹ The building called temple of Craticula was a little west of the Porticus of Octavia. See *Ordo Romanus*, Extract 1. The region of *Arenula* (Rione della Regola) appears to have been also called *regio caccabariorum*, and the church now S. Maria de Pianto to have been S. Salvatore Cacabari. (Cencius,

At the Antonine Bridge, the Ring of Antoninus;[2] where is now Saint Mary in Caterino. At Saint Stephen *in Piscina* (that is to say, at the Cistern)[3] the palace of the prefect Chromatius, and a temple that was called *Holovitreum*, being made of glass and gold by mathematical craft, where was an astronomy with all the signs of the heavens, the which was destroyed by Saint Sebastian with Tiburtius, the son of Chromatius.

in Mabillon, *Mus. Ital.* 193; Martinelli, *Roma Sacra*, 388); *Nomina ecclesiarum saec. xiv.* Urlichs, *Codex*, 170, 174). This church is said to have been at the entrance of the 'temple of Craticula.' *Anon. Magliab.* Urlichs, *Codex*, 169.

[2] *Circus* [al. *arcus*] *Antonini*. In the list of Theatres, part i. c. 8, we have the theatre of Antoninus by the bridge of Antoninus. The same monument is doubtless meant here, probably the theatre of Balbus. If so, the church of S. Maria *in Catarino* [al. *Cataneo*] cannot be identified with S. Catarina de Rota. Martinelli, *Roma Sacra*, 371.

[3] The church of S. Stefano *in piscinula* stood opposite to S. Lucia in the Via S. Lucia. Chromatius (*Praefectus urbis*, A.D. 284) was known by the *Acta* of St. Sebastian, in which his palace and its destruction are described. (*Acta Sanctorum*, Bolland. 10 Jan.) See *Ordo Romanus*, Extract 4.

16. *Of the Tranſtiberim.*

IN *Tranſtiberim*, that is to ſay, beyond Tiber, where is now Saint Mary, was the temple of the Ravennates, where oil flowed from the earth in the time of the emperor Octavian; and there was the *taberna meritoria*,[4] where the ſoldiers ſerved for wages, that waited without pay in the ſenate.[5] Beneath *Janiculus*, the temple of the Gorgon.[6] At the river ſtrand, where

---

[4] The name *urbs Ravennatium*,—which occurs in ſome of the Acts of Martyrs, and which has been thought to be derived from ſome *caſtra Ravennatium* eſtabliſhed in the Traſtevere, analogous to the *caſtra Miſenatium* in the Third Region,—ſuggeſted to the writer a 'temple of the Ravennates' on the ſite of S. Maria in Traſtevere. The legend of the fountain of oil and the name *taberna meritoria* are from the chronicle of Jerome. *Anno Abrah.* 1976, *E taberna meritoria trans Tiberim oleum terra erupit fluxitque tota die ſine intermiſſione, ſignificans Chriſti gratiam ex gentibus.*

[5] *Ubi merebantur milites qui gratis ſerviebant in ſenatu.*

[6] *Templum Gorgonis.* In the Notitia, Region XIV. *Tranſtiberina*, a monument called *Caput Gorgonis* is regiſtered.

the ships do tarry, the temple of Hercules. At the Cistern⁷ the temple of Fortune and Diana. In the Licaonian island⁸ the temple of Jupiter and the temple of Æsculapius, †and the body of the apostle Saint Bartholomew.†

Without the Appian Gate, the temple of Mars, and a Triumphal Arch.⁹

⁷ *In piscina.* There is a little church between the island and S. Cecilia, called S. Benedetto *in Piscinula* (*in Piscina*, Cencius in Mabillon, *Mus. Ital.* ii. 193), where St. Benedict is said to have lived (Martinelli, *Roma Sacra*, 79). The temple of Fors Fortuna *trans Tiberim* was probably known to the author through Ovid (*Fasti*, vi. 773), but this appears to have been outside the Ostian Gate. Becker, *Handbuch*, i. 479

⁸ The name, *insula Lycaonia*, occurs in some of the *Acta Martyrum*. The temples of Aesculapius and of Jupiter are associated by Ovid, (*Fasti*, i. 291):

Accepit Phœbo nymphaque Coronide natum
    Insula, dividua quam premit amnis aqua.
Iupiter in parte est; cepit locus unus utrumque,
    Iunctaque sunt magno templa nepotis avo.

⁹ See pp. 10, 29, and notes 20, 62. This paragraph appears to be out of place, or the commencement of a new chapter on objects without the walls.

17. Conclusion.

THESE and many more temples and palaces of emperors, confuls, fenators and prefects were in the time of the heathen within this Roman city, even as we have read in old chronicles, and have feen with our eyes, and have heard tell of ancient men. And moreover, how great was their beauty in gold, and filver, and brafs, and ivory, and precious ftones, we have endeavoured us in writing, as well as we could, to bring back to the remembrance of mankind.

MIRABILIANA.

MIRABILIANA.

1. The Marvels of Roman Churches, A.D. 1375.[250]

1. *Of the Founding of the Church of Saint Mary Major.*

JOHANNES Patricius, senator of the city, let make the church of Saint Mary Major; likewise also did pope Liberius. For, on the same night, whiles they slept, Our Lady Mary appeared unto them, saying, I lay upon you this commandment, that ye build me a minster. And when as in the morning they were come together, taking counsel concerning the marvel by them seen, by the one as by the other, that they should dedicate a church in honour of the blessed Virgin,

---

[250] The following imperfect description of the ecclesiastical Marvels of Rome, the Latin text of which is printed by Parthey, as part of the *Mirabilia*, from a manuscript of the fourteenth century (Codex Vatic. 4265; Parthey, *Mirabilia*, pp. 47-62), has been thought worth reproducing here as a supplement to that work. The text is incomplete in many places; and some words are for this or other reasons occasionally omitted in the English version.

there came messengers, which showed unto them, how that snow had fallen in one place, the season being in May time. They therefore acknowledged this miracle, and dedicated a church in that place. And it is therefore called Mary Major, because the snow fell in the midst of May.[1]

2. *Of the Conversion of Constantine.*[2]

CONSTANTINE, that was emperor, caused male infants to be brought, that he might be bathed in their blood, after the advice of his

---

[1] The church of S. Maria Maggiore was called S. Maria *ad Præsepe* after its most famous relic, and S. Maria *ad Nives* from the miraculous fall of snow, which is usually said to have occurred on the 5th of August, on which day the feast of its dedication is kept. (Pet. de Natalibus, *Vita Sanctorum*, f. 136; Baronius, *Martyrolog.* 5 Aug.) The month given here is founded apparently upon a fanciful derivation of the title *Major*.

[2] The story of the baptism of Constantine by St. Silvester appears in the Greek Acts of Silvester, attributed to the sixth century. The legend as here narrated is found in the medieval legendaries. It is painted on the wall of the transepts of the Lateran Basilica, and in the chapel of St. Silvester at the Quattro SS. Coronati; and is alluded to by Dante (*Inferno*, xxvii. 94),

> Ma come Costantin chiese Silvestro
> Dentro Siratte a guerir delle lebbre.

physicians and doctors, to the intent that he
should be cleansed of his leprosy. But the apostles Peter and Paul appeared at night unto him
in his dreams, and bade him send to the pope of
the Christians, the holy Silvester, who then lay
hidden in Mount Syrapte. Wherefore a message
was sent to that place. Silvester, when he saw
those knights [draw near, supposed that they
came to summon him to his] death [3] . . . . . .
He, coming to Constantine, showed him a picture
in the likeness of the Apostles, and asked him,
whether they that appeared to him in the night
were like unto that picture, and he said that it
was even so. The picture yet standeth in the
altar-wall above the high altar.[4] Constantine
therefore was baptized, the idols of Rome were
beaten down, and the emperor in his baptism
was also healed by Silvester of his leprosy.
Nevertheless there remained of his sickness, upon
his forehead, one little spot, by reason of one idol,
that he held dear, and had hidden it away.
And when he found that he had the spot by
reason of the hidden idol, he destroyed the same,

---

[3] *Militibus illis visis cum mortem.* The text is
defective, and some words are supplied. So Peter
de Natalibus: *Qui videns milites credidit se ad martyrium
evocari. Acta S. Silvestri,* f. 20.

[4] At St. John Lateran, p. 132.

and so was healed. Constantine gave ... ass or horse,[4] and a red mitre that Peter had as pope;[5] and he brought him with ... bridle on a horse to the Lateran. Now his mother Helen disputed with her son of his conversion. And the same had been beyond sea; and she brought with her two wizards. .. The ox falls [upon the word] of Helen's wizards, and rises again by the prayers of Silvester.[6] It was after this fight that Helen passed beyond sea for to win the Holy Cross.

[4] *Dedit az^m asinum aut equum.*

[5] The *mitra* or *regnum* (see p. 68, note 124) which Silvester was believed to have received from Constantine, was taken to Avignon, and, having been brought back to Rome, was restored by Eugenius IV. to the Lateran, from whence it was stolen in the time of Innocent VIII. Rosponi, *de Basilica Lateranensi*, 195.

[6] *Bos cadit ... incantatorum Elene (?) resurgit per orationes Silvestri.* The story here alluded to is told in the legendaries. Helen had embraced Judaism, and to assist her in the religious controversy, brought with her some Hebrew advisers, one of whom, being a wizard, whispered a word into the ear of a fierce bull, which killed him. Silvester spoke the name of Christ, and the bull arose tame. Pet. de Natalibus, *Acta Constantini*, f. 20.

3. *Of the Basilica of Saint Peter.*

IN Saint Peter's of Rome, as one first goeth into his minster, is the first altar, whereat Saint Peter celebrated mass. And as you go on further, in the great door of the same minster lieth the Venerable Bede.[7] In the inside to the left behind the sepultures of the popes, is the altar of Saint Gregory, wherein his body is laid;[8] from whence stretcheth the Vatican Way in the half behind the Sacristy, proceeding along it toward the nave of the minster.[9] . . . After the altar

---

[7] *Venerabilis Beda.* The memorial of Beda consisted of a disk of porphyry lying under the silver door, afterwards replaced by the bronze doors of Pope Eugenius IV., which now close the principal entrance of the modern basilica. The English Beda was erroneously believed to be buried here. Another Beda, a monk of the monastery of Gavello near Rovigo, contemporary of Charlemagne, had the reputation of sanctity. His relics were translated to Genoa. *Vita Bedae iun.* cum notis Papebroch. in *Acta Sanctorum*, Bolland. 10 April, p. 866; Mabillon, *Mus. Ital.* i. 142.

[8] The chapel of St. Gregory the Great, built by Pope Gregory IV. was in the south-east corner to the left of the entrance. De Angelis, *Basilica Vaticana*, Plan.

[9] *A quo protenditur via Vaticana in medietate* (?) *post sacristiam procedendo iuxta eam versus navem monas-*

of Saint Gregory is the chapel of Peter and Paul, where are the first wooden images made after the likeness of the same apostles. . . . Thereafter is interposed a certain . . . . . a great altar, in the midst of which lyeth John Chrysostom, and nigh to the same door is the altar of Saint Alexius; and it is said that his body is laid before the same altar under the lamp that hangeth there, and that in his own church no more is had of Saint Alexius but his head. And above the same altar is an image of the blessed Virgin . . . made by Saint Luke. Behind this, beneath the Sacrifty, is Saint Peter's chair.[260] Beyond in the midst, is the high altar of Saint Peter, where none but the pope alone was wont to sing mass,[1] beneath the which altar is one half of the relics of the bodies of Saint Peter and Saint Paul, and there is the *sessorium* of Saint Peter.[2]

---

terii via Lavicana. I cannot explain what sense is concealed here.

[260] *Posthoc sub sacriftia est capud seu cathedra sancti Petri.*

[1] *Ubi nullus nisi solus papa conjuevit celebrare.* The past tense shows that the work belongs to the time of the residence of the popes at Avignon, that is, between 1311 and 1378, and confirms the date, 1375, given in the last page.

[2] *Et ibidem sessorium sancti Petri.* The relics of the Apostles were, and are, in the *Confessio* under

Thereafter is the altar of Saint Crofs in a chapel, where of old time, in a certain window behind the altar, oil did iſſue forth, and the ſtone is ſhown that is ſet there and pitted with holes.³ Into that chapel women enter not by the ſame reaſon, becauſe a certain woman, when the ſaid oil, that had healed many ſick folk, ſtained her robe, did curſe the oil, and thereupon the ſame ceaſed to drop. Therefore that woman, and all the women that yet do enter the ſaid chapel, are accurſed and excommunicate.

Thereafter is the chapel of Saint John Baptiſt, where is the baptiſtery,⁴ wherein men were wont to be chriſtened at certain times of the year; and it was reſolved that thoſe baptiſms ſhould be removed from that place unto Saint John of Lateran.⁵ Then before the pope's palace is the

the high altar. The pope on the third Sunday in Advent uſed to go down and perform a ſervice in the *Confeſſio*, ſitting *in ſubſellio*. *Ordo Romanus Benedicti*, in Mabillon, *Mus. Ital.* ii. 122.

³ *Et oſtendit* [qu. *oſtenditur*] *lapis ibidem poſitus et foraminibus feneſtratus*. The oratory of St. Crofs was to the right of the high altar.

⁴ *In qua eſt baptiſmus*.

⁵ *Et conjultum fuit de iſto loco fundi* (qu.) *baptiſmus in ſanctum Johannem Lateran*. The ceremony of the baptiſm of adults takes place at the Lateran on Eaſter Eve.

Holy Rood of Christ's blood. There is the altar . . .

As one entereth first into the same church, to the right is the altar of *Veronica*, above which the Vernicle is enclosed.⁶ Into the same as one entereth, toward the left, in the wall above is the cross of Saint Peter, nigh whereunto rest the bodies of the Apostles.⁷ Then further, towards the left, is the Vatican, where many popes and many saints do rest.

In the same church is one of the thirty pieces of silver. Also, an image of the Holy Majesty, which spake to King Charles, saying, My son, thou has offered to all, but to me hast thou given nothing. Charles therefore drew from his finger a ring, and cast it to the wall, where the same noble stone is yet seen; but he himself fell to the ground and worshipped.⁸ In the same place yet . . . in the stones from the feet and for the head.⁹

There is also the church of Saint Andrew and

---

⁶ The altar of Veronica was in the north-east corner of the old basilica to the right of the entrance.

⁷ I suppose the apostles Simon and Jude.

⁸ I do not know whether this story refers to Charlemagne, who was especially liberal in his gifts of money and jewels to the church of St. Peter.

⁹ *Ibidem adhuc . . . . in lapidibus a pedibus et a capite.*

the minster of Saint Parnel.²⁷⁰ Moreover there is the image of Christ, from whose head a head fell.¹ Also nigh unto the altar where the pope consecrateth the emperor, hangeth the Cord of Judas Iscariot. There are twenty and eight degrees before the church, like as at Saint Gregory by the Seven Floors.² There also at the side is laid the body [of Christ] that was changed into a finger in the hands of the blessed Gregory.³

4. *Of the Church of Lateran.*

IN the Lateran, before the ambit, is the seat of the dung-heap,⁴ where the pope is led for to sit, when he hath been crowned at St. Peter's;

---

²⁷⁰ See pp. 70, 71.

¹ *De cuius copite cecidit caput.*

² *Iuxta septemsolium.* See note 70.

³ *Item est positum corpus in latere.* According to the legend, St. Gregory was administering the body of Christ to a lady, who was incredulous, because she recognised the bread as part of her own offering. On the prayer of Gregory, the bread was changed in form to part of a finger with blood on it, and then changed again to bread. *Acta S. Gregorii*, Mombritius, i. 330.

⁴ *Sedes sterquilinii.* This ceremony is described in the *Ordo Romanus* of Cencius, and in that of Jacobus Gaietanus. In the former, written in the

and he faith: Silver and gold have I none, but that I have, give I thee. Above the palace before Saint Silvefter[5] be two feats, in the which it is confidered, whether the pope be a man or woman.

In the fame place is an image of the Majefty [6]

---

time of Celeftine III. (1191-1198), the *fedes ftercoraria* is faid to be *ante porticum bafilicae Salvatoris patriarchatus Lateranenfis;* in the latter, about 1320, it is defcribed as *fedes marmorea ante porticum nunc deftructam.* Mabillon, *Mus. Ital.* ii. 211, 259.

[5] *Ante fanctum fanctorum* [read *Silveftrum*]. The two feats here alluded to were before the bafilica of St. Silvefter at the Lateran Palace, and the pope on the day of his coronation fat firft on one, and then on the other. While in the firft he received the keys of the Lateran palace and bafilica. From the fecond he threw money to the people. Both feats were of porphyry. (Mabillon, *Mus. Ital.* ii. 212, 261; Crefcembeni, *S. Giovanni avanti Porta Latina,* p. 140.) We fee above the popular interpretation of thefe fingular ceremonies. Leo X. was the laft pope in whofe coronation they were ufed. All the three feats were preferved in Mabillon's time in the cloifter. The *fedes ftercoraria* was not *perforata.* (Mabillon, *Mus. Ital.* i. Pref.) As to the legend of Pope Joan, with which the ftory in the text is connected, fee p. 139.

[6] *Ymago maieftatis proiecta in lapide ecu cum lapide vulnerata eft fanguinea a tefferatore.* I cannot difentangle the words of the text; but Cencius fays, that on the arch of the bafilica of St. Silvefter was

.... There is a crofs that paffed from wall to wall by reafon of the words of a certain prieft, which gave abfolution of a fin to a woman that confeffed unto him.

In the chapel that is called *Sancta Sanctorum*,[7] is well nigh all of the Coat without Seam, whereof the other part is in the greater Church .... where the altar top is the Lord's table in the Supper.[8] Moreover, in the fame church or chapel be the heads of the apoftles[9] Peter and Paul, and a picture of the Saviour, which, being ftruck in the forehead by a Jew, dropped blood, as might ftill be feen. (Mabillon, *Mus. Ital.* ii. 212.) A ftain of blood was fhown on one of the fteps of Pilate's houfe (the Scala Santa) formerly at the chapel of St. Silvefter, now before the Sancta Sanctorum. Crefcembeni, *Chiefa S. Giovanni avanti Porta Latina*, 140.

[7] The Sancta Sanctorum was the chapel of St. Laurence, and is ftill preferved.

[8] *In ecclefia mayori argenteo in cuius ecclefie cacumen altaris eft menfa domini in cena.* The Coat without feam was one of the relics at the high altar, where was alfo the wooden altar of the Martyrs in a filver frame, and, above that, the table at which the Laft Supper was celebrated. See the Table of Lateran Relics printed at the end of the volume.

[9] *In eadem ecclefia five capella funt capita apoftolorum.* Thefe heads were placed by Nicolas III. in the Sancta Sanctorum, but were transferred by Urban V in 1369 to the high altar, and placed in

the head of Saint Agnes, and the head of Saint [Euphemia], and a part of Chrift's body, that Chrift confecrated in the Supper, and many other things befide. Alfo above, under a vault,²⁸⁰ is an image of the Majefty, painted by God's hand, the which the bleffed Luke had drawn in the picture. Alfo before the Holy of Holies is the image of Our Lady, before which Theophilus was reconciled.¹ In the fame place is the head of Zachary.²

Moreover, above the high altar in the church, is the table with the images of the apoftles Peter and Paul, which was fhewed unto the emperor Conftantine by grace divine.³

---

the two filver bufts which are now in the upper part of the ciborium. Rofponi, *Bas. Lateran*, 45.

²⁸⁰ *Item fuperius in teftudine.* This famous picture of the Saviour, painted on wood, is above the back of the altar in the Sancta Sanctorum under an arched gothic canopy of marble.

¹ Parthey writes *antequam Theophilus reconciliatus fuit.* I do not know what ftory is alluded to.

² *Caput Zathae* [read *Zachariae*]. In one lift of relics at the Lateran is the head of Zacharias the Prophet; in another the head of Zacharias, father of St. John Baptift; but neither is defcribed as being in the Holy of Holies. Crefcembeni, *S. Giovanni avanti Porta Latina*, 136, 139; compare Mabillon, *Mus. Ital.* 570.

³ See p. 123.

In another part is the veffel, wherein Conftantine was baptized and cleanfed from leprofy, before the chapel of Saint John Baptift, wherein women enter not. In . . . . is another chapel, wherein is painted an image of Our Lady, that upon the offering of a ring by a certain woman, ftretched forth her hand and drew to her the ring, where it yet appeareth upon the finger in the picture.

5. *Of Saint Paul's Bafilica, and the Cloifter of Anaftatius.*

IN Saint Paul is the other moiety of the bodies of the apoftles Peter and Paul; and the great chalice of Pope Honorius, where be written verfes to this purport:[4]

> Paul of high name, take this noble veffel,
> Which I, Honorius, who prefide in the Sacred Court, give in thine honour,
> That thou in anfwer to pious prayers mayeft give me thy realms of piety,
> And that I may feek the reft of peace and be united with the bleffed.

[4] *Nominis excelfi, vas nobile fufcipe, Paule:
Vas in honore tu[o do] prefful Honorius aulæ,
Ut tua regna piis precibus michi des pietatis,
Et fatur pacis requiem, iungarque beatis.*
Poffibly the fecond word in the laft line was *feder*.

At Anaftafius is a cloifter of Ciftercian monks at the Salvian well,[5] where be three wells. . . . . There was the bleſſed Paul beheaded; and when he was beheaded, he cried thrice: Jeſus, Jeſus, Jeſus; and in each place a well flowed, after the three leaps of the head.

6. *Of the Churches of Saint Mary Major, and the Round Saint Mary.*

IN Saint Mary Major above the high altar is an image of the face of Chriſt, with another picture, that was not made by man, but by the hand of God. There is alſo the image of the bleſſed Virgin by the hand of God, but as ſhe ſat to be painted by Saint Luke. In the ſame church lyeth Saint Jerome; alſo the cloak left at Troas,[6] whereof the apoſtle maketh mention in his Epiſtle. There be alſo three long ſplinters of Our Lord's Crofs, and ſome of the milk of the bleſſed Virgin, and Our Lord's blood in a

---

In the third line the tranſlator has ſubſtituted *des* for *dis*, and in the ſecond has added the letters within brackets.

[5] *Ad fontem ſalinum* [qu. *ſalvinum*]. Aqua Salvia; ſee p. 30.

[6] The Latin copy has *aula et cuſtoitium*, for which the tranſlator has read *penula relicta Troadi*.

cryftal, and of the wood of the Holy Crofs; the head of the apoftle Saint Matthias, whofe body alfo refts before the altar.[7] Nigh unto Saint Mary Major, Simon Magus began his flight, and before New Saint Mary he fell.[8]

At the church of Round Saint Mary [9] [the porch] hath one hundred feet of width, and four-fcore and four feet of depth.

7. *Of the Church of Saint Mary New.*

IN New Saint Mary is a table wherein is painted by Saint Luke, as it is faid, the image of Saint Mary with her child; and upon a time when that church was burned, this table alfo was fet on fire,[290] and was blackened all over,

---

[7] The place of depofit of the body of St. Matthias appears to have been uncertain in the twelfth century. See Johannes Diaconus, in Mabillon, *Mus. Ital.* ii. 573.

[8] As to the legend of the flight of Simon Magus, fee the next chapter.

[9] *In ecclefia fanéte marie rotunde.* The meafurement here given appears to be that of the portico, the external dimenfions of the whole fquare addition to the Rotunda being 112 × 84 Englifh feet. Taylor and Crefy, *Monuments of Rome*, plates 45, 46.

[290] *Ifta tabula est et abigna* [read *ufta ab igne*] *fuit.*

and nought doth appear either of the garments or of the limbs, but the faces of the mother and child did endure unhurt, as yet appeareth.[1] In the same at an altar is the stone that is marked by the kneeling of Saint Paul,[2] when he prayed during the flight of Simon Magus, who fell before that church, where the place is marked on the stones.[3] Thereby is the temple of Peace, wherein it was written, I shall not fall but if a maid bear a child, and again, The temple shall not fall except a maid bear a child.[4]

[1] The picture is still shown.

[2] St Peter and St. Paul are associated in this miracle. Gregory of Tours says that the stones indented by the knees of the apostles remained, and that the rain-water collected out of those holes healed the sick. (Gregor. Turon. *de glor. mart.* i. 28, cited Urlichs, *Codex*, 185.) A stone with two holes is still shown in the church.

[3] The place where Simon fell was believed to be marked in the fourteenth century by a stain on the pavement. *Cernet lapidem infando Simonis cerebro maculatum.* (Petrarch, *Epist. Fam.* ix. 13, ed. 1853). An early legendary speaks of four stones united into one by the broken body. Urlichs, *Cod.* 181.

[4] The temple, or palace, of Romulus of the *Mirabilia* (pp. 20, 100) has become the temple of Peace, by which name it continued to be known for many centuries.

8. *Of divers Churches and Relics.*

NIGH to Saint Hadrian, and against that image of stone,⁵ is the Prison of Saint Peter, and a well in the same. Moreover, the pillars whereunto the apostles were bound, are at Saint Mary Transpontina;⁶ where is the place in which Saint Peter was crucified.⁷

At Saint Peter *ad vincula* is the chain wherewith he was bound. At Saint Paul is Saint Paul's chain.

At Round Saint Mary⁸ is Saint Agnes *in Agone*, where she was cast forth and set in a brothel.

At Saint Silvester, where be the nuns of Saint Clare, is shown Saint John Baptist his head.⁹

At Saint Pudentian, sister of Praxed, are the

---

⁵ *Contra illam ymaginem lapideam.* The image of Marforio.

⁶ *Apud sanctum Marcum in cropediem* [read *sanctam Mariam Transpadinam.*] The pillars were in the old church of S. Maria Transpontina (frequently miswritten Transpadina), and in 1587 were carried in procession to the new. (*Roma Antica et Moderna*, 1668, p. 88.)

⁷ See notes 142, 144.

⁸ That is, near the Pantheon, in Piazza Navona.

⁹ This famous relic, from which the church had the name of S. Silvestro *in capite*, is not now there, but is preserved at the Vatican.

T

bodies of Pudentian and Priscilla, and there was the cemetery of Priscilla; also the place of baptism of the same virgins. There was their father's house, the dwelling-place of Peter and Paul.[300]

Where Crispin is and Crispinian, is the pastoral staff of the same.[1]

In Saint Praxed is the body of Saint Maurice and his forty fellows.[2] Moreover in Saint Praxed is the body of the same saint; and the third part of the column whereat Christ was scourged, in a small chapel, where women enter not.

From Saint Praxed, as one goeth toward Saint Sixtus, towards the left, are the Thermae of Dio-

---

[300] *Ibi fuit domus paterna Petri et Pauli.* The house of Pudens, the father of Pudentiana and Praxedes, at which St. Peter was received as a guest.

[1] The bodies of SS. Crispin and Crispinian are said to have been brought from Scissons to Rome, and entombed at St. Laurence in Panisperna. (Baronius, *Martyrologium*, Oct. 25) But neither of them was a bishop.

[2] The more popular Saint Maurice of the Theban Legion has been substituted by the author, or his copyist, for an obscure Roman martyr, Maurus. The ancient list (inscribed on a marble table in the church) of saints, whose bodies to the number of 2,300 were transferred from the catacombs by Pope Paschal I. and placed under the high altar at S. Prassede, includes the following: *Mauri et aliorum quadraginta martyrum.*

cletian, which were painted by the Four Crowned Martyrs;³ and in the same way is a memorial of the Geese, that roused the Romans from sleep and freed them from captivity.

In going from Saint Sixtus is the castle of Antonianus, under which is the castle of the Three Legions.⁴

9. *Of Pope Joan.*⁵

MOREOVER nigh unto the Colosseum, in the open place,⁶ lieth an image which is called the Woman Pope with the boy, whose

---

³ There may be a confusion between the Thermae of Diocletian and those of Caracalla; but even so the description of the direction is unintelligible.

⁴ *Castrum Anthoniani sub quo est castrum trium* (?) *legionum.* The first are probably the *thermae Antoninianae.*

⁵ The fabulous Pope Joan was said to have succeeded Leo IV. who died in 855, and to have filled the see of St. Peter for more than two years. The legend makes its first appearance in the thirteenth century (Martinus Polonus, *Chronicon,* ed. Plantin. p. 317), and was generally believed until the end of the fifteenth.

⁶ *In platea.* In the Mantuan plan published by De Rossi (*Piante di Roma*), the *loco dove parturì la papessa* is shown to the north of S. Clemente,

body is buried at Saint Pitreus *in bonio*.⁷ Moreover, in the fame open place is a Majefty of the Lord, that fpake to her as fhe paffed, and faid: In comfort fhalt thou not pafs;⁸ and when fhe paffed, fhe was taken with pains, and caft forth the child from her womb. Wherefore the Pope to this day fhall not pafs by that way.⁹

apparently towards the end of the Via Labicana. But in Panvinius' note to Platina (*Vitae Pontificum*, 101b, 104) it is implied that the *facellum*, then ftill exifting, where the female pope was faid to have been buried, was not in the Via Labicana, but in the other way from the Coloffeum to S. Clemente, which ran between the Via Labicana and the road paffing the SS. Quattro. It fhould be obferved that in the twelfth century, before the legend of the female pope was current, there was a *domus Iohannis papae* between the Coloffeum and S. Clemente. Cencius, *Ordo Romanus*, c.29, in Mabillon, *Mus. Ital.* vol. ii.

⁷ *Ad fanctum Pitreum in bonio.*

⁸ *Comodo* (?) *non tranfibis.*

⁹ The ancient proceffional routes between the Lateran and the Coloffeum are defcribed in the *Ordo Romanus*, Extract 4. It is poffible that at a later time, when the legend was current, the fpot affociated with it was purpofely avoided. See the note of Panvinius, in Platina, *Vit. Pontif.* 104. At the date of the text, the papal proceffions had long been difcontinued owing to the abfence of the popes. See note 261.

10. *Of Ara Celi, and Saint Sixtus.*

AT Saint Mary in Ara Celi [210] is an image, painted by God's hand, of the blessed Virgin in tears, as she stood by the cross.

In Saint Sixtus [is the minster] of the Friars Preachers and holy Nuns; there be the bodies of Pope Zephyrinus, of Pope Lucian, of Pope Soter, of Calocerus and Parthenius, of Pope Lucius, of Lucius bishop and of Maximus martyr;[1] and an image of the blessed Virgin made by Saint Luke;[2] the which a certain pope obtained by wrong, or took away, and carried the same into the Holy of Holies, saying that the mother ought to be with the Son, whose image is there. But in the morning, against the dawn, the image returned with a great light to the worship of the Sisters; and the same in the Holy Week changeth his colour, so

---

[210] *Ad sanctam Mariam mamma celi.*

[1] *Ibidem sunt corpora pape Severini pape Luciani pape Persutheris pape Calethorii pape Perthoquinii pape Luci episcopi Maximii martyris.* The names in the translation are corrected from the table in the church (Martinelli, *Roma Sacra*, 306). But the name of Lucian is not in the list of popes.

[2] This miraculous picture, placed by St. Dominic himself in S. Sisto, was transferred with the nuns to the church of SS. Domenico e Sisto on the Quirinal Hill.

that on Good Friday it is all pale. In the same place is . . . . the table of the blessed Dominic, upon which the angels brought bread; and the altar whereat the same saint sang Mass, and raised from the dead the Cardinal's nephew, by whose means he hath many monasteries in England.[4]

11. *Of the things beyond Saint Sixtus.*

FROM Saint Sixtus in going toward Saint Sebastian, when you come to the wall, is the Latin gate, where is a cloister to the left,[b]

---

[4] The miraculous cure by St. Dominic of a young kinsman of the Cardinal of Fossa Nova, who was thrown from his horse and brought lifeless into the house, is narrated in the life of the Saint. (Mombritius, *Acta S. Dominici*, i. 245b.) The Cardinal was Stephen de Ceccano, Abbot of Fossa Nova in Campania, who was created Cardinal 1211, and died 1227. His young kinsman, according to Ciaconio, was his brother's son, Napoleon, but is called by others Napoleon Orsini. The Cardinal held by King John's gift the church of Bamburgh in Northumberland, out of which he assigned to the nuns of S. Sisto a pension of fifty marks, redeemed in 1428. Ciaconius, *Vit. Pontif.* i. 646; *Taxatio P. Nic. IV.* 317; *Bull. Ord. Praedic. an.* 1244, 1428, Add. MSS. Brit. Mus. 15,352, p. 118.

[b] *Ubi est claustrum* [read *claustrum*] *ad sinistram*. The church of St. John *ad portam Latinam* was anciently a collegiate church of secular canons

and there is the vessel wherein Saint John the Evangelist was set, and the chain that he was bound withal; and there nigh before the gate, on the right hand, as one goeth forth, is the place where Saint John was set in the vessel of boiling oil.

And as one goeth further without the walls, toward Saint Sebastian, in the Appian Way, is the chapel *Domine quo vadis;* and a conduit.

12. *Of the Palatine, and Saint Gregory.*

AT the Greater Palace is the Garden of Delights, and Ovid's Palace. There is also the cloister of the holy Gregory, wherein he let make him a monk; in the same cloister is a book of Dialogues of his hand, and there is the image of the Crucifix, that nodded his head to bear witness between a Jew and a Christian, of the money received. At the same is the board, whereat Saint Gregory did set twelve poor folk whom he had bidden, and our Lord Jesus Christ appeared as the thirteenth guest. Near by is the cloister of Saints John and Paul, martyrs, where their bodies do rest.

under an Archpriest. In 1144 it was united to the Lateran Basilica, but appears to have preserved its collegiate character. Crescembeni, *S. Giovanni avanti Porta Latina,* 224, 246.

13. Of sundry Churches and Relics.

AT Saint Vivian is her head, where rest four thousand martyrs.

At Saint Marcellus is the head of Saint Cosmas.

At Saint Paul's Gate is the Sudary of the same Saint.[7]

At Saint Alexius is the head of Alexius, and the head of Saint Boniface.

At Saint Cicely is her head; and there was her house, and her body is there in the altar, with nine hundred and six other bodies.

Saint Silvester bound the dragon, that had slain of Romans more than can be told, in the end of

---

[7] *Ad portam sancti Pauli est sudarium domini* [read *ejusdem sancti*]. The *sudarium domini* would be the Vernicle, preserved at St. Peter's. Probably the object here alluded to was the kerchief (*velum*), said to have been borrowed by St. Paul on the way to his own martyrdom, and miraculously restored to St. Plautilla (or Lemobia) at the moment of his death. (Mombritius, *Acta Sanctorum*, f. 194 b; P. de Natalibus, *Acta S. Pauli*.) The place where it was restored was shown outside the Ostian Gate. Perhaps the kerchief itself was exhibited in a chapel there. See note 456 on the medieval Plan of Rome at the end of this volume.

the Greater Palace, where now is the church of Saint Mary of Hell.⁸

There be two places where holy martyrs suffered in the city: at Saint Vitus *in macello*⁹ near Saint Mary Major, and at Saint Sebaftian.³²⁰

At the Holy Angel in the Fifh market, is Saint Felicity with her feven fons.

In Saint Bartholomew in the Ifland is fhown his head; and there alfo is his body under a golden bull of the emperor.¹ There alfo is the head and body of Paulinus, confeffor and bifhop. Moreover, there is the arm of Thaddeus, the arm of Simon, and the chin of Saint James the Greater.

At Saint Crofs in Jerufalem.² . . . . . There

---

⁸ See p. 97, 98.

⁹ The church of S. Vito was at the ancient *Macellum Liviae* (see *Ordo Romanus*, Extract 3), but was called *ad macellum martyrum*, and a ftone was fhown there on which many martyrs were believed to have been put to death.

³²⁰ St. Sebaftian on the Palatine, near the Stadium, the place of martyrdom of that faint.

¹ Both the emperors Otho II. and Otho III. are faid to have brought to Rome from Benevento the body of St. Bartholomew; but the poffeffion of this relic was ftill difputed by the Beneventines. See Baronius, *Martyrologium*, Aug. 25; Gregorovius, *Hiftory* (Ital. Tranfl.), iii. 584.

² *Ad Sanctam Crucem in Ierufalem ibi quedam*

moreover, is the cord wherewith Chrift was bound on the crofs;[3] alfo Chrift's fponge, and one of the nails of Chrift's crucifixion with eleven thorns of his Crown; and there in the tower without, put away in the wall, was that golden fcripture that Pilate wrote over the head of Chrift: *Jefus of Nazareth King of Jews.* There is alfo one great timber, that hangeth above in the great minfter, of the crofs of the thief that hung on his right hand.[4]

Near by is the ciftern of fome emperor, the

---

fecit fe demorari aut demembrari. Perhaps the words here corrupted or loft referred to the building of the church by St. Helena in a place where fhe was believed to have dwelt.

[3] *Ligatus fuit ad ftatuam.* The laft word appears to be corrupt. An ancient infcription from the lower chapel printed by Martinelli, fays: *funis quo ligatus fuit D. N. Iefus Chriftus in Cruce. Roma Sacra,* 96.

[4] *Unum magnum lignum . . . de cruce dextri lateris ac latronis.* The penitent thief became in medieval legend Saint Difmas. *S. Difmas fuit ille latro qui a dextris domini crucifixus eft.* P. de Natalibus, f. 65.

  In that Chirche is alfo
  Of the Croys he was on-do,
  That heng on Rode him by,
  And of his funnes hedde Merci.

The Stacions of Rome (Early Englifh Text Society, 1867), p. 13.

which he had always full of wine; and now Saint Angel's church is there.⁵ On the other side, towards Saint John in Lateran, is Pilate's house.⁶

At Saint Mark's is his robe with many other relics.⁷

At Saint George *ad velum aureum* is his head.

At Saint Laurence *in Panisperna* Saint Laurence was broiled, and there is his fat in a cryſtal, and the iron wherewith he was ſtirred.

---

⁵ I cannot find any notice of a church of S. Angelo in this locality, nor explain the alluſion to the ciſtern. Is it poſſible, that the amphitheatre included in the wall may have been called by the pilgrims the Emperor's wine-vat? Compare note 141.

⁶ The Scala Santa and ſome columns at the Lateran Palace were ſaid to be part of the houſe of Pilate.

⁷ The church of St. Mark was built by, and named after St. Mark, Pope and Confeſſor, whoſe body was transferred thither in 1145. The *veſtis* mentioned in the text may be aſſigned to Mark the Evangeliſt.

14. *Of the Churches in Tranftiberim.*

AT Saint Mary in *Tranftiberim*, outfide the church, did oil flow forth three days when Chrift was born.⁸ Moreover, there is an image of the blefled Virgin aloft above the door, which anfwered unto the Romans, that they were fafe by reafon of the penance that they had done. In the fame is the body of Saint Calixtus.

In the church of the Holy Ghoft is the body of Saint Cyriac; and in a chapel above, in the hill in Nero's Camp,⁹ is an image of the blefled Virgin, which Saint Luke did make.

In Saint Chryfogonus is the body of the fame Saint, and the arm of Saint James the Greater, with many other relics.

In Saint Cicely is her body.

15. *Of the Aventine Hill.*

IN Saint Sabba's minfter, which he founded, lie Titus and Vefpafian and Volufian.³³⁰

---

⁸ See p. 115.

⁹ Perhaps the little church of St. Michael *in Saffia*.

³³⁰ In the Portico of St. Sabba, there is faid to have been a great fepulchral ftone with an infcription beginning thus:

Conditur hic tumulo Titus cum Vefpafiano.

The Aventine Churches.

In Saint Prisca is her body; also the bodies of Aquila and Priscilla, of whom the Apostle wrote.

In . . . an altar[1] that was consecrated by Pope Gregory, to whom, as he sang mass at the same, appeared an image of Christ crucified; in remembrance whereof Pope Urban [ordained] the office *Nos autem*; and over the same altar is a picture of Saint Luke of his own hand.[2] And there is the holy sandal of Saint Peter. Also a small piece of the Chair of the same.[3]

16. *Of St. Barbara, St. Martin, and St. Agnes.*

IN the church of Saint Barbara is her head and arm; also the pillar whereunto she was bound with her sister.

In Saint Martin in the Mount is the body of Saint Silvester pope.

At Saint Agnes without the walls, there is

(Martinelli, *Roma Sacra*, 296.) Volusian was associated with Titus in the legendary story of the punishment of the Jews for the killing of Christ. See note 36.

[1] *In altare.* Perhaps we should read, *In sancta Balbina est altare.* That church was consecrated by St. Gregory. Martinelli, *Roma Sacra*, 76.

[2] *Pictura sancte* (sic) *Luce de manu propria.*

[3] *Item in* [?] *ejusdem Cathedra* [?] *parva peccia.*

over the altar an image of Saint Agnes, holding in her hand the ring, that she received from John, her priest, by the order of Pancasius,[4] as yet appeareth. In that convent there was one that should be cloistered, but she could not; and at the last she confessed the cause; wherefore they that be in that cloister cannot abide but if they be clean maids.[5] In the same place is the head of Constantia, and of Amata,[6] virgins.

[4] *Quam recepit a presbytero Iohanne ex iussu Pancasii.* This story is alluded to by Petrarch in a letter to Philip de Vetriaco: *Videbit Agnetis annuulm et divinitus extinctae libidinis miraculum recognoscet* (Petrarch, *Ep. Fam.* ix. 13. ed. Le Monnier, 1853). A priest of her church begged leave of the Pope to marry. The Pope gave him a ring, and bade him ask St. Agnes to take him as her spouse. He offered the ring to the statue of the Saint, which extended its finger and clasped the ring; and the priest had no inclination for any other wedlock. (*Acta Sanctorum*, Bolland. 10 Apr.) The priest in the legend is called Paulinus, the name of the pope is not given.

[5] At St. Agnes was a convent of nuns until 1499, when Sixtus IV. removed them, and put the church under the care of the Canons Regular of St. Saviour. Martinelli, *Roma Sacra*, 52.

[6] *Amate.* Perhaps St. Emerentiana.

17. *Of Saint Laurence.*

AT Saint Laurence in Lucina is his gridiron and the chain that he was bound withal.

There is his body and that of Stephen protomartyr,[7] and the stone whereupon Saint Laurence was put, when he was lifted off from the gridiron. And the body of Hippolytus below in a chapel, in an altar.

In Saint Laurence [*in fonte*] is his prison and a well therein.[8]

18. *Of Saint Sebastian.*

AT Saint Sebastian is the Cemetery of Saint Calixtus at the Catacombs. And without is the *campus agonis*, wherein is an idol, at the which Saint Sebastian was shot with arrows. And near by is the well, wherein Saint Urban baptized . . . and his hiding-place. And in Saint Sebastian is Pope Stephen, and the place where he was beheaded. In the same is the woman of

---

[7] This paragraph applies to St. Laurence without the Walls.

[8] St. Laurence *in fonte*, in the Via Urbana, is said to have been the house of St. Hippolytus. Martinelli, *Roma Sacra*, 137.

Samaria.⁹ And in going into Saint Sebaftian appear the ftones of Saint Stephen.³⁴⁰ Alfo two croffes in a lamp which are faid to have been made before Our Lord became flefh. There alfo in a field, over againft Saint Sebaftian, nigh to his chapel, is a well, out of which [Saint Urban] chriftened Saint Cicely and Tiburtius and Valerian.¹

. . . . . ² In the church of Saint Peter *ad Vincula* is very remiffion of all fins.

In the year of Our Lord M.CCC.LXX.V.³

---

⁹ The head of the woman of Samaria appears to have been one of the relics at St. Paul without the Walls. *Roma Antica e Moderna,* 1668, p. 20.

³⁴⁰ *Apparent lapides de fanéto Stephano.* Probably the ftones marked the place of Pope Stephen's martyrdom. He was killed while celebrating mafs at the cemetery of Lucina : *cuius fanguis in pavimento effufus adhuc ibidem apparet.* Petrus de Natalibus, f. 134 b.

¹ This feems to be the fame well as that mentioned above.

² In this place in the manufcript are copied fome Indulgences granted by Pope Gregory to Roman Churches. Parthey, *Mirabilia,* 62.

³ See note 261.

II. A DESCRIPTION OF ROME BY BENJAMIN OF TUDELA, A HEBREW TRAVELLER, ABOUT A.D. 1170.[4]

ROME is divided into two parts by the river of Tiber, the one part being on one fide, and the other part on the other. In the firft part is a right great temple, that is called Saint Peter's of Rome, and there alfo is the palace of the great Julius Cæfar;[5] and there, moreover, are full many buildings and works, the like whereunto are not in the world. And around the part of

[4] The Hebrew book, from which the above defcription is extracted, has been printed in a Latin Tranflation at Antwerp in 1575, and again at Leyden in 1633, in an Englifh Tranflation by Wright (*Early Travels in Palefine*, London, 1848), and in a German tranflation by Martinet at Bamberg in 1858. Not having Mr. Wright's work at hand, I have taken the above from a later Latin tranflation by Dr. Geiger, given in the valuable *Codex Topographicus* of my friend, Prof. Urlichs, p. 178.

[5] *Mirabilia*, pp. 22.

Rome wherein men dwell, are spread out twenty and four miles of ruins.⁶ And there be found therein eighty Palaces of eighty full mighty kings, that be all called emperors from Tarquin's reign unto the reign of Pepin son of Charles, who first conquered Spain, when it was holden of the Ishmaelites. The Palace of Titus is without Rome,⁷ who was not received by the three hundred Senators, because he had not fulfilled their commandment, and had not taken Jerusalem until the third year, whereas they had set him to do it in two years. Moreover there is the palace of Vespasian, after the manner of a castle, a right great building and a strong.⁸ There also is the palace of king Malgalbinus, in whose palace be three hundred and three score houses, after the number of days in the year, the compass whereof reacheth unto three miles.⁹ And whereas upon a time war arose among them, more than an hundred thousand men were slain in this palace, whose bones are hung there unto this day; and

⁶ *Mirabilia*, p. 6.

⁷ *Mirabilia*, p. 22.

⁸ Perhaps the Colosseum.

⁹ Urlichs suggests the catacombs Compare *Mirabilia*, p. 29. May it not be the *Palatium majus*, the vast ruins of the Palatine? The carved work seems to allude to the sculptures of the Arch of Severus, or the imperial columns.

the Emperor set forth in carved work all that had happened in that war, how faction was set against faction, host against host, men and horses with their armour, all in marble, for to show unto them that came after how great a war had once been. Moreover is found there a cave under ground, where the Emperor and the Empress his wife sit on thrones, and an hundred barons of his realm stand around, all embalmed with drugs unto this day.[350]

And there be there, in Saint John's church at the Latin Gate, at the altar, two brazen pillars of the works of King Solomon, to whom be peace; and in each of them is cut the inscription, Solomon Son of David;[1] and it was told unto me by Jews abiding in Rome, that every year on the ninth day of the month Abib, a sweat like unto water droppeth from those pillars. And there is there a crypt, or privy chamber, wherein Titus, son of Vespasian, did hide the holy vessels taken from Jerusalem.[2]

There is also another crypt, in a hill by the shore of the river Tiber, wherein be buried the

---

[350] Perhaps the Mausoleum of Augustus. *Mirabilia*, pp. 80, 81.

[1] *Mirabilia*, p. 66, note 119. St. John at the Latin Gate is put for St. John Lateran.

[2] *Mirabilia*, p. 65.

ten righteous men of blessed memory,[3] who were slain under the reign of . . . .

Moreover, before the basilica of the Lateran is Samson carved in stone, holding a globe in his hand. Then there is Absolon, son of David,[4] and the Emperor Constantine, who built the city that is called after his name Constantinople; whose image with his horse is of gilded brass. There be moreover other buildings and works in Rome, the number whereof no man can tell.

---

[3] This appears to refer to ten doctors of the Mishna, who were killed between the time of Vespasian and Hadrian. Wright, *Early Travels in Palestine*, 68, cited by Urlichs, *Codex*, 179.

[4] It is uncertain what statue was known to the Jews by this name. As to Samson, see *Mirabilia*, p. 64.

MIRABILIANA.

III. Ordo Romanus.[355]

Extract 1. *Proceſſion from Saint Anaſtaſia to the Vatican, part of the Ceremony of Chriſtmas-day.* (Mabillon, *Muſeum Italicum*, ii. 125. *Ordo Romanus*, c. 16.)

IN the morning the Pontiff ſaith Maſs at Saint Anaſtaſia, which done, he goeth down with proceſſion by the way nigh to *Porticus Galla-*

---

[355] The following extracts are taken from the *Politicus Benedicti Canonici*, a treatiſe on the religious ceremonial of the Papal Court, written by Benedict, a Canon of St. Peter's, and dedicated to Guido de Caſtello, Cardinal of St. Mark. The latter became pope in 1143 under the name of Celeſtine II. The book muſt therefore have been written before that date. It has been already ſhown in the Preface, how the *Politicus* was aſſociated with the *Mirabilia* in the century which produced them both. The paſſages relating to proceſſions, which are tranſlated in the following extracts, furniſh the moſt important evidence reſpecting the medieval topography of Rome, and are eſſential to the inter-

torum,⁶ before the Temple of the Sibyl, and between the temple of Cicero and *Porticus Crinorum;*⁷ and proceeding between the basilica of Jupiter and the Flaminian Ring,⁸ he then goeth nigh to the Severian Porch, and crossing before

pretation of the *Mirabilia*. The *Politicus* of Benedict is printed with other Ritual Books, under the general title of *Ordo Romanus*, in Mabillon, *Museum Italicum*, vol. ii.

⁶ A record of the year 1243 mentions some houses *in porticu Gallatorum ante ecclesiam S. Marie de Gradellis* (Nerini, *S. Alessio*, 432). As to this church, and the temples of the Sibyl, and of Cicero, see pp. 111, 112.

⁷ The temple of Cicero being at S. Niccolo *in Carcere* or *in carcere Tulliano*, the *Porticus Crinorum* must be placed between this and the Capitoline hill; perhaps the ancient *porticus* of the Forum Olitorium.

⁸ *Circum Flaminium*. (So Urlichs from Cod. Vatican. 5348; Mabillon has *arcum Flaminium*). In going from the church of St Nicolas to the Porticus of Octavia, the most important monument, which the procession must have passed, was the Theatre of Marcellus. It is probable that the name of the Flaminian Circus had been transferred to the ruin of this theatre, which seems to have been included in the stronghold of Pierleone. See p. 23, note 44; p. 113, note 238. The basilica, or temple, of Jupiter was in the *Porticus Octaviae*. See p. 112. The way would pass between this and

the temple of Craticula,⁹ and before the *infula
milicena et draconariorum*,³⁶⁰ fo on the left hand
goeth down to the Greater Way of Arenula,¹
paffing by the Theatre of Antoninus;² and by the
Palace of Cromatius, where was the *Holovitreum*,³
and under the arch of the emperors Gratian
Theodofius and Valentinian,⁴ he entereth by the
Bridge of Hadrian before his temple, and nigh
unto the obelifk of Nero,⁵ and before the memorial
of Romulus,⁶ and by the *Porticus* afcendeth into
the Vatican to the bafilica of Saint Peter, where
is a ftation; and mafs is there fung with all the

the theatre, and then in front of the *Porticus*, on
the entablature of which was, and is, the infcription
of Severus.

⁹ *Mirabilia*, p. 113, note 241.

³⁶⁰ *Infula melicena* (al. *militena*) *et draconariorum*.
This *infula* appears to be a group of houfes like the
infula argentaria (see *Mirabilia*, p. 92). In the fame
Ordo (chapter 22) the *draconarii* are mentioned
among the officers affifting in papal ceremonies.

¹ The Via della Regola.

² *Tranfiens per theatrum Antonini*. Probably the
theatre of Balbus. See p. 23.

³ *Per palatium Cromatii ubi fuit olivitreum*. See
note 243.

⁴ See p. 10, note 19.

⁵ See p. 114.

⁶ See p. 75. The *Porticus* was the covered
way through the Borgo to St. Peters.

Orders of the Palace as behoveth; and he should there receive the crown on his head, and return with procession through the midst of the city to the Palace, to finish the festival of the Crown.

2. *Procession from Saint Hadrian to Saint Mary the Greater, part of the Ceremony of the Feast of the Purification of the Blessed Virgin.* (Ib. c. 29, p. 131.)

IN the morning station at Saint Mary the Greater. The eighteen images of the deacons[7] issue forth, and with the clerks and people they go to Saint Hadrian, where a collect is done. But my lord Pontiff dismounteth at Saint Martina with the bishops and cardinals and the other schools. Then with the rest he is robed ... Then he walketh to Saint Hadrian, where is a stational cross. ... Then the sub-deacon taketh up the stational cross; and when he cometh forth he raiseth it, and carrieth it before the Pontiff in procession unto Saint Mary the

---

[7] *Exeunt xviii. imagines a diaconis.* So in the same *Ordo*, cap. 29, *cum xviii. imaginibus diaconorum.* There were at that time eighteen *diaconiae*, the incumbents of which were the Cardinal Deacons, but in this document they are simply called *diaconi*, and the Cardinal Priests *cardinales*.

Greater. The *primicerius* on the left hand, supporting the pallium of the Pontiff, singeth with the fingers the anthem *Adorna thalamum tuum Sion.*

The Pontiff with the others faith Pfalms, and so proceeding bare-foot before the arch of Nerva, he entereth by the Forum of Trajan, and going forth of the Arch of *Aurea* in the *porticus apsidata*,[8] ascendeth by the hill nigh unto

[8] *Et sic procedens discalciatus ante arcum Nervae* (?) *intrat per forum Traiani et exiens arcum aureae in porticu apsidata.* Jordan understands the procession to have gone first in the direction of the Arch of Nerva (that is, the arch adjoining the temple of Minerva in the Forum Transitorium), then to have turned to the left through the Forum of Augustus (included in that of Trajan, see note 186), and to have gone out of the imperial Fora through the Arco dei Pantani. (Jordan, *Topographie*, ii. 474). But this interpretation gives a forced sense to the words *et sic procedens ante arcum*, which, according to the usage observed elsewhere, should mean passing by the object, not walking towards it. It is probable that the words *arcum Nervae* conceal a reference to some other monument near S. Adriano. Jordan suggests *arcam Noe;* but if this name was then popularly applied, as it was in the fifteenth century, to the temple of Minerva (Urlichs, *Codex*, 165, 225), it would scarcely be employed by a learned writer, who in another place calls the same building the temple of Nerva, see p. 171. One

Eudoxia,[9] and crossing by the *silex* nigh to the House of Orpheus,[370] goeth down by the title of Saint Praxed to Saint Mary the Greater.

may suspect that the monument really passed was the ruin with Doric pilasters near S. Adriano described by Labacco and destroyed in the sixteenth century (Note 190). I am inclined to think that the route is the same as that shortly described in Extract iv, and the *arcus Aureae* (if that is the true reading, compare p. 167) *in porticu apsidata* is the Arch of the Forum Transitorium, which appears to have opened into a curved porticus. (See the plan in Middleton's *Ancient Rome*, 253.) There is reason to think that the Arco dei Pantani was closed through the middle age. It is so represented in Bufalini's plan; the existing marks of rafters on the arch show that medieval buildings were placed against it; and the *Anonymus Magliabecchianus* describes the monastery of St. Basil as extending to the temple of Minerva (Urlichs, *Codex*, 165). The expression *per Forum Traiani* does not, according to the usage of the author, necessarily mean *through*, but rather *along the side of*, the Forum. See note 384.

[9] *Iuxta Eudoxiam.* Near S. Pietro in Vincoli, called *Titulus Eudoxiae*. *Mirabilia*, Part ii. c. 6.

[370] The church of S. Lucia *in Orphea*, otherwise called S. Lucia *in silicis*, had its name from a *lacus Orphei* (probably a fountain adorned with sculpture relating to Orpheus), mentioned in the *Notitia*, Region V.

3. *Procession from Saint Mary the Greater to the Lateran on Easter Day, with the ceremony of the Last Supper.* (Ib. c. 48, p. 141.)

MASS ended (at Saint Mary the Greater) the Pontiff is crowned, and returneth with procession to the Palace by the Esquiline Hill. Entering under the arch, where it is called the Livian market,[1] he proceedeth before the temple of Marius, that is called *Cimbrum*,[2] crossing by *Merulana*, goeth up to the palace by the Fullery.[3] In the entry of the basilica of Saint Zacchary Pope, after receiving the lauds of the cardinals and judges, as in other crown-days,[4] he dismounteth from his horse, and is received by the *Primicerius*. The *Secundicerius* of the judges taketh the crown, and giveth it to the chamberlain,[5] who placeth it with care in the chest. And on that day the Judges bring him into the great Leonian basilica, into a chamber where eleven benches are prepared and one lower seat[6] around

---

[1] The arch of Gallienus by the church of St. Vitus *in macello*, on the site of the ancient *macellum Liviae*.

[2] *Mirabilia*, p. 107.

[3] *Iuxta fulloniam.* See p. 79.

[4] *In aliis coronis.*

[5] *Cubiculario.*

[6] *Undecim scamna et unum subsellium.*

the table of my Lord Pontiff, as well as his own couch [7] well arranged, after the fashion of the Twelve Apostles around Christ's table, when they did eat the Passover. There five Cardinals and five Deacons and the *Primicerius* recline on their elbows at supper, the *presbyterium* having been first given in the chamber with the *manus*,[8] as on Christmas day. The Pontiff then ariseth and cometh to the place that is called *Cubitorium*, where the roasted lamb is blessed; and blesseth it, and returneth to the couch at the table. The Prior of the basilica sitteth in the lower seat before the couch. Then my lord Pontiff taketh a little of the lamb, and first offereth it to the Prior, saying: That thou doest, do quickly, and as Judas received unto damnation, so do thou receive unto remission; and putteth the same into his mouth, who taketh and eateth. The rest of the

[7] *Lectus.*

[8] The *presbyterium* and the *manus* appear to have been gifts of money. In cap. 22 it is said, "On Christmas day and on Easter day he giveth to all the principal officers (*omnibus prioribus*) a *manus*, that is a double *presbyterium*, to wit to the Prefect xx *sol.* and the *manus*, to the primicerius of the judges iiii. *sol.* and the *manus*, to each of the judges iiii. *sol.*, etc. So after the greater Litanies (c. 56) the clergy receive from the Curia of my lord Pope a *presbyterium*.

lamb he giveth to thofe that fit at meat with him, and to others as he will, and fo they all do eat. And when the banquet is half done, a deacon arifeth on the bidding of the archdeacon and readeth the Leflon. The fingers then by the order of my lord Pontiff fing a Sequence fuitable for Eafter with the mufic of the organ ; and that done, they go and kifs the Pontiff's feet, who giveth them a cup full of liquor,⁹ the which they drink, and receive from the Burfer³⁸⁰ one bezant.

4. *Proceffion from the Lateran to Saint Peter's and back, part of the Ceremony of Eafter Monday.* (Ib. c. 50, 51, p. 143.)

IN the morning all the Orders Palatine are affembled at the palace with the Pontiff, and come down from the palace ; and my lord Pontiff rideth. He entreth by the Field¹ near Saint Gregory *in Martio*,² goeth down into the

⁹ *Coppam plenam potione.*
²⁸⁰ *A faccellario.*

¹ The *campus Lateranus*, called in Bufalini's plan *campus fanctus*, lay to the north of the Bafilica and Palace.

² S. Gregory *in Martio* is identified with the little chapel of S. Maria Imperatrice, which lately

Greater Way, under the Conduit Arch, and on the right hand before Saint Clement,* turning to the left near the Coloſſeum, paſſing by the arch of

exiſted in the garden of the Engliſh ſculptor, Warrington Wood, at the Villa Campana, in the angle between the Via S. Giovanni Laterano and the Via SS. Quattro.

* *Deſcendit in viam Maiorem ſub arcu formae et dextra manu ante ſanctum Clementem.* According to an ancient document, cited by Maringoni from the Regiſter of the Hoſpital of St. Michael (or St. Saviour), the way leading from S. Stefano Rotondo to the Lateran was called *via maior et ſancta* (Maringoni, *Sancta Sanctorum*, 291; Urlichs, *Codex*, 186). Adopting this interpretation of *via maior*, the proceſſion, for a ſhort diſtance, followed that road, which lay to the ſouth of the aqueduct; then paſſed under one of its arches and took a way (now no longer exiſting) on the right hand, leading to the front of the atrium of S. Clemente; after paſſing which it turned to the left (into the via Labicana) and paſſed along the north ſide of the Coloſſeum in the direction of the Via Tor de' Conti. The whole route may be traced on Bufalini's plan. But it is perhaps more probable that the *via maior* of the Ordo was the road to S. Clemente repreſented by the preſent Via di S. Giovanni (Urlichs, *Codex*, 90), in which caſe the proceſſion, having entered that route under one of the arches of the aqueduct, turned to the right to paſs before the atrium of S. Clemente.

Aurea [4] before the Forum of Trajan as far as Saint Bafil, and going up by the hill about the *Militiae Tiberianae*,[5] goeth down by Saint Abbacyrus,[6] and paffing before the Holy Apoftles, on the left hand going down into the *Via Lata*, and turning down by the *Via Quirinalis*,[7] and pro-

[4] *Tranſiens per arcum Aureae* [al. *Nerviae*]. Whatever is the true reading, the arch is probably that which formerly ſtood to the ſouth of the temple of Minerva in the Forum Tranſitorium. See p. 162. It is important to obſerve that the word *per*, in the language of this document, does not mean *through* or *under*, but *by*. When the proceſſion paſſes through an arch, the expreſſion is *ſub arcu*. See notes 383, 401, 403. The proceſſion therefore does not enter the imperial Fora, but continues outſide the wall of the Forum of Auguſtus (in which was eſtabliſhed the convent of St. Bafil), towards the Torre delle Milizie.

[5] *Circa militias Tiberianas*.

[6] This church (originally dedicated to S. Cirus *abbas*, converted by a gradual corruption to *S. Abbacyrus*, and Santa Pacera) appears to have been near the north end of the hemicycle of the Forum of Trajan, by the Via Magnanapoli. See Martinelli, *Roma Sacra*, 332, 335.

[7] *Siniſtra manu deſcendens in via Lata* [qu. *viam Latam*] *et declinans per viam Quirinalem*. The *Via Lata* is the Corſo. The *Via Quirinalis* (not known as an ancient ſtreet) was evidently a ſtreet leading from the Quirinal hill acroſs the Corſo; poſſibly

ceeding to Saint Mary *in Aquiro* at the Arch of Pity,⁸ fo goeth up to the *Campus Martius*,⁹ paffing before Saint Trifo,³⁹⁰ nigh to the Pofterns,¹ unto the Bridge of Hadrian; entreth by the bridge, and goeth forth by the *Porta Collina*² before the temple and caftle of Hadrian, proceeding before the obelifk of Nero, entreth by the Porch nigh to the Sepulchre of Romulus,³ goeth up to the Vatican, into the bafilica⁴ of the bleffed Apoftle Peter; and there fingeth mafs with all the Roman People.

the lane leading from the *Trivium* (Piazza Trevi) towards the Pantheon, or the ftreet mentioned by Petrarch as crofing the Via Lata, *ubi tranfverfa illam* (*Viam Latam*) *fecat via, quae a montibus ad Camilli arcum, et inde ad Tiberim defcendit* (Petrarcha, *Epift. Famil.* viii. i.) For the Arch of Camillus, fee p. 21, note 40.

⁸ See p. 14, note 28; and p. 84.

⁹ See p. 84, note 162.

³⁹⁰ The church of S. Trifone faced the Via della Scrofa, and was abforbed in the convent of S. Agoftino.

¹ *Iuxta pofterulas.* Thefe appear to have been openings in the wall, which was carried along the bank of the river from the corner near the Porta Flaminia to the Aelian Bridge.

² The Porta Collina occurs in the lift of Gates, *Mirabilia*, p. 8. It appears to have clofed the bridge from the Leonine City.

³ *Mirabilia*, Part iii. chapter 3.

⁴ *In bafilica* [read *bafilicam*].

The which ended, he is crowned before the
bafilica of Saint Peter, in the place where he
mounteth his horfe; and wearing his crown he
returneth with proceffion to the Palace, by the
fame Holy Way⁵ by the Porch and by the aforefaid bridge, entering under the triumphal arch
of the emperors Theodofius, Valentinian and
Gratian,⁶ and goeth nigh to the palace of Cromatius, where the Jews make praife.⁷ Preffing
on by Parione between the Ring of Alexander⁸
and Pompey's Theatre, he goeth down by
Agrippa's Porch and goeth up by the *Pinea*,
nigh unto *Palatina*,⁹ and paffing on before Saint
Mark, goeth up under the Arch of the Hand of

⁵ *Per hanc viam facram.*
⁶ *Mirabilia*, p. 10.
⁷ *Mirabilia*, p. 114. In the *Ordo Romanus* of
Jac. Gaietanus, the place where the Jews made
their reverence to the pope is faid to be *ad turrim
de Campo*. Mabillon, *Mus. Ital.* ii. 259.
⁸ *Profilicus per Parionem inter circum Alexandri*
etc. Between the Piazza Navona and the theatre
of Pompey. The *Porticus Agrippina* is probably the
Portico of the Pantheon, infcribed with the name of
Agrippa.
⁹ *Afcendit per pineam iuxta palatinam.* The name
of *Pinea* remains in the Piazza Pigna, and is ftill
attached to the Region. The bafilica of St. Mark
was founded, A D. 336, by St. Mark Pope, *iuxta Pala-
tinas. Lib. Pontif.* 49.

Flesh, by the *Clivus Argentarius*[400] between the *insula* of that name and the Capitol, goeth down before the prison of Mamertinus, entreth under the Triumphal Arch,[1] between the Fatal Temple and the Temple of Concord,[2] proceeding between the Forum of Trajan and the Forum of Cæsar, entereth under the Arch of Nerva,[3] between the

---

[400] *Sub arcu manus carneae per clivium argentarium.* See pp. 12, 91, 92.

[1] *Intrat sub arcu*, etc. This may serve as evidence, that in the earlier part of the twelfth century one vault at least of the Arch of Severus was still open. At the end of the same century it appears by a bull of Pope Innocent III. (*Mirabiliana*, part iv.) that the south vault belonged to the clergy of St. Servius, and the middle vault, which was divided between them and a private proprietor, was already occupied by chambers.

[2] The Fatal temple was Sta Martina. The temple of Concord was rightly known. (See page 95).

[3] *Sub arcu Nervae*, [*Nerviae*, Mabillon]. Leaving the arch of Severus, the procession goes through the ancient *Forum Transitorium*, having on the left hand the ' Forum of Trajan' which included that of Augustus (see p. 92), and on the right the so-called Forum of Cæsar (see p. 99), and passes *under* the arch between the temple of Minerva and another building (possibly the Colonnacce) called the temple of Janus. But this arch appears to be called elsewhere *arcus Aureae*. See pp. 161, 167.

temple of the same goddess and the temple of Janus, goeth up before *Asylum* along the *silex* where Simon Magus fell before the Temple of Romulus,[4] proceedeth under the Triumphal Arch of Titus and Vespasian which is called the Seven Lamps, goeth down to the *Meta Sudans* before the Triumphal Arch of Constantine, turning on the left hand before the Amphitheatre,[5] and by the Holy Way nigh unto the Colosseum [6] returneth to the Lateran; and there being honorably received, and praises having been made by the cardinals and judges, goeth up to the Palace; giveth a *presbyterium* without *manus*,[7] and maketh a banquet [8] in the same Leonine Basilica. After the banquet he goeth down to Vespers, and doth the office as it is written.

[1] See pp. 100, 136.

[5] *Reclinans manu laeva ante amphitheatrum*.

[6] *Per sanctam viam iuxta Coloseum*. The *sancta via* may be the road passing by SS. Quattro. See Panvinius, in Platina, *Vit. Pont.* f. 104. But in the document cited in note 383 it is identified with *via major* and the lane passing by S. Stefano Rotondo.

[7] *Presbyterium sine manibus*. See note 398.

[8] *Celebrat convivium*.

5. *Procession from the Coloffeum to Saint Peter's, in a Greater Litany.* (Ib. c. 57, 58, p. 146.)

WHEN the proceffion is come before the Colofieum, the Subdeacon of the Region beginneth the Septiform Litany, and they of the bafilicas [9] fing the refponfes unto the feventh. And when he is come before Saint Mary New, my lord Pope, in a bed prepared for the purpofe,[410] taketh reft, with the Bifhops, Cardinals and Deacons, until the Litany be ended. The which done, my lord arifeth and faith, *Oremus*, and the Deacon, *Flectamus genua*. The refponfe foundeth, *Levate*. The Pontiff faith a prayer; the deacon, *Procedamus cum pace*, and they all return in proceffion by the *via facra*[1] to the before-mentioned *Clivus Argentarii*, or Silverfmith's Hill. The Subdeacon beginneth the Quinqueform Litany in the fame order as before as far as the bed before Saint Mark, where my lord repofeth, as in the firft. Then they return in proceffion to the Triumphal Arch of the Emperors Theodofius,

---

[9] *Bafilicarii*.

[410] *In praeparato lecto*.

[1] *Per viam Sacram*. The ufe of the claffical name in this inftance is remarkable. The name was preferved in the Acts of Saints. Compare *Mirabilia*, note 195.

Valentinian and Gratian,[2] where he beginneth the Triform Litany as far as the bed on the Hadrian Bridge. They then come to Saint Laurence in the Greater Porch,[3] where he beginneth the Simple Litany as far as the bed at the *Cantarus* before Saint Mary of the Vergers at the end of the Court.[4]

The Litany ended and the other offices, he ascendeth to the basilica of Saint Peter, where is a station, and there my lord Pontiff singeth Mass.

6. *Procession with the Sacred Picture, part of the Ceremony on the Feast of the Assumption of St. Mary.* (ib. c. 72, p. 151.)

IN the Assumption of Saint Mary, my lord Pope, with all the *Curia*, doeth Vespers and Vigils of nine lessons in the church of Saint Mary Greater. When this is done, he returneth to the Lateran, and the Cardinals and Deacons,

---

[2] See pp. 10, 159.

[3] St. Laurence, also called *in Piscibus* from a family of that name (Martinelli, *Roma Sacra*, 365), is in the Borgo S. Michele, now included in the Borgo San Spirito.

[4] *Usque ad lectum cantari ante sanctum Mariam in Virgari* [al. *Virgariorum*] *in fine cortinae.* The

with all the people, take the image of Jesus Christ from the Basilica of Saint Laurence,[5] carrying it through the Lateran Field nigh to the basilica of Saint Gregory.[6] . . . The prefect, with the Twelve Men, receiveth from the *Curia* twelve torches;[7] and the Ushers twelve more, which they carry kindled before the Image. While the Image passeth through the Field, the chamberlains stand on the top of Saint Gregory,[8] holding two kindled torches, the which they quench when the Image is passed. And when the Image is come to Saint Mary New, they put it down before the church, and wash his feet with basil.[9] Meantime, in the church, the Schools do

---

cantarus here mentioned was not the fountain in the Parvise (p. 73), but another basin at the foot of the steps of St. Peter's, before a chapel which took its name from the chaplains who attended with rods at the high altar (*virgarii*), and who had an *hospitium* near this chapel. Martinelli, *Roma Sacra*, 375.

[5] The famous picture in the chapel of St. Laurence or Sancta Sanctorum. See p. 152.

[6] See p. 165.

[7] *Faculas.*

[8] *In culmine sancti Georgii* [read *Gregorii*].

[9] *Lavant pedes eius de basilico.* That is, with water in which this herb was steeped. The water so used was believed to acquire a healing power. *Aqua illa qua cum basilico pedes eius lavantur a languentibus hausta nonnullis extat causa recuperandae salutis.*

Matins, to wit, of three Lessons.⁴²⁰ And the people standing and blessing the Lord, take the Image thence and carry it to Saint Hadrian, where they wash his feet. And, issuing from the church, they return by the way they came, and carry it by the Arch *in Lathone*,[1] because of old time there was a great persecution of the Devil there. Then they pass nigh to the House of Orpheus, by reason of the Basilisk, which at that time lay hid[2] there in a hole, by whose stench and hissing men that passed thereby were made sick and died: therefore Pope Sergius ordained this Procession in this great festival, to the intent that by the lauds of so many people, and the intercession with God of the most holy Virgin Mary, the Roman people might be delivered from these persecutions.

They then go up to Saint Mary where my lord Pontiff, being arrayed, singeth Mass, and blesseth the tired people; and they all depart.

Lateran MS. cited by Martinelli, *Roma Sacra*, 158.

⁴²⁰ *Trium scilicet lectionum.*

[1] *Arcum in Lathone.* See p. 100, note 203.

[2] *Iuxta domum Orphei propter basiliscum qui tunc temporis latitabat.* See note 370. The basilisk may be the dragon of the legend of St. Silvester, or perhaps another monster. *Mirabilia*, p. 98.

IV. THREE RECORDS.[423]

1. *Grant of the Capitoline Hill to the Abbey of St. Mary in the Capitol. Extract from a Bull of Pope Anaclete II. (about 1130) cited in a Bull of Pope Innocent IV. 1252.*[b]

ANACLETE Bishop, Servant of the Servants of God, to his beloved sons in Christ, John, Abbat of the Holy Mother of God

---

[423] The extracts here translated furnish examples of the two kinds of documents from which a complete commentary on the *Mirabilia* would be largely drawn, namely, legal records and ecclesiastical inscriptions. The two Bulls throw light on the medieval topography of the most interesting parts of Rome, the Capitol and the Forum. The List of Relics of the Lateran is inserted in illustration of the passages in the *Mirabilia* (p. 65), and in *Church Marvels* (p. 131), relating to the same subject.

[b] These Bulls are printed in Casimiro, *Storia della chiesa di Araceli*, pp. 21, 432. The Bull of Anaclete, which is of a date between 1130 and 1134, is extracted in Urlichs, *Codex*, 147; Jordan, *Topographie*, ii. 667.

and Virgin Mary, and of Saint John Baptist in the Capitol, and his successors to be regularly promoted for ever .... To the said monastery of the same Mother of God, to thee committed, We do grant and confirm the whole hill of the Capitol in entirety, with the houses, crypts, cells, courts, gardens, and trees, both fruitful and unfruitful, together with the *porticus* of the Camellaria,[5] with the land before the monastery that is called the Market-place,[6] with the walls, stones, and columns, and all things in general thereto appertaining; the which is included in these bounds: on the first side is the Public Way that leadeth by the Silversmith's Hill, that is now called the Descent of Leo Prothus:[7] on the second side is the Public Way that leadeth under the Capitol; and from thence it goeth down

---

[5] The Porticus of the Tabularium overlooking the Forum appears to have been called *Camellaria*, or *Camellaria superior* to distinguish it from a building (constructed in the cell of the temple of Concord and belonging to the clergy of the church of St. Sergius) which is called *Camellaria inferior* in a Bull of Innocent III. 1199 (p. 181), and *Cameliana S. Sergii* in a Bull of Innocent VI. 1360 (Martinelli, *Roma Sacra*, 390). See *Mirabilia*, p. 90.

[6] *Qui locus nundinarum vocatur.* See *Mirabilia*, pp. 88, 89; Casimiro, *Storia di Araceli*, 433.

[7] The Salita di Marforio.

through the boundary and hillside,⁸ above the gardens which Ildebrand and John de Guinizo did hold, as far as the Greater Temple that looketh over the Elephant:⁹ on the third side are the banks that are over the Well of the Meat-Market,¹³⁰ and thence winding by their cliffs¹ above Canaparia,² as far as the charnel-house of Saint Theodore:³ on the fourth side it goeth up from the same charnel-house through the hole where is the Versified Stone,⁴ and thence goeth

---

⁸ *Exinde descendit per limitem et appendicem.* The sense seems to require *ascendit*, as the boundary is carried up from the lane at the foot of the hill (under Ara Celi) to the ruins on the edge of the hill over Piazza Montanara. The word *appendicem* appears to be used in the same sense as the modern Italian *pendice*.

⁹ *Mirablia*, p. 88, note 171.

¹³⁰ *Fontem de macello*, probably in the Piazza Montanara.

¹ *Per appendices suas.*

² *Mirabilia*, pp. 96, 97, note 196. In a list of churches, enumerated in order, by Niccolo Signorili (Cod. Vat. 3536), the following names occur in this order, *S. Adriani, S. Martinae, SS. Sergii et Bacchi, S. Mariae de Canapara, S. Mariae de Inferno.* Casimiro, *Ara Celi,* 438.

³ *In carnarium S. Theodori.*

⁴ *Per cavcam in qua est petra versificata.* An inscribed stone; possibly the architrave, rediscovered

down by the Garden of Saint Sergius[5] to the Garden that is under the Camellaria, coming by the Hundred Steps[6] to the firſt bound: around the ſame Hill we do grant and confirm to thee and thy ſucceſſors the houſes, crypts, and ſhops in the Market, and all the Hill of the Capitol in entirety, and all other things that are in the hill or about the hill.

2. *Grant to the Church of St. Sergius and Bacchus, of half the Arch of Severus and other property. Extract from a Bull of Pope Innocent III. 1199.*

TO Romanus Archprieſt and the clerks of the Holy Martyrs Sergius and Bacchus, as well preſent as future for ever.

Albeit the care of all churches[7] is committed

in the fifteenth century, with inſcriptions relating to the ſo-called *ſchola Xanthi*.

[5] This garden was behind the church of S. Sergius. Compare the next record extracted.

[6] *Per Gradus centum.* Apparently the aſcent to the Capitol from the Priſon. An aſcent to the Capitol called *Centum Gradus* is mentioned by Tacitus (Hiſt. iii. 71); but is not neceſſarily the ſame.

[7] *Licet omnium ecclesiarum.* The firſt part of the bull, preceding the deſcription of the property,

to us, nevertheless it behoveth us the more diligently to provide for those that are in the City and to keep their rights unimpaired, inasmuch as they are known more especially to belong to our jurisdiction .... we do grant .... the moiety of the Triumphal Arch, which in all consists of three arches, whereof one of the lesser arches is more near to your church, upon which arch one of the towers is seen to be built; and the moiety of the greater arch that is in the middle, with the chambers next to the lesser arch; with their entrances and exits and all their appurtenances, which are included under these bounds. On the first side is the other moiety of the same Triumphal Arch, of the right of the heirs of Ciminus; on the second side is another close[8] of the above-written Ciminus, and a court and the public way; on the third side is the court of your church; and on the fourth side is the public way which passeth before the said church, as in the instrument of demise made by Gregory, of good memory, to the Cardinal Deacon of the same church is more fully contained; the church of St.

is not fully given in the collection of the *Regesta Innocentii III.* i. 404. The description of the property is extracted in Latin by Jordan, *Topographie*, ii. 668.

[8] *Aliud claustrum.*

Saviour *de statera*,[9] with its appurtenances; the church of Saint Laurence, situate under the Capitol, with the buildings,[440] crypts, gardens, and all other appurtenances thereof; all the houses situate *in Gallicis* which are included in these bounds; on two sides it is held by your church, on the third side it is held by Saint Martina, on the fourth side is the public way which passeth before the said church; .... an house situate near the house of John de Ascesa; four crypts with the tofts[1] before them, as far as the public way behind the church of Saint Saviour de Statera, which ye bought of the heirs of Peter de Ascesa; one toft in the region of Saint Theodore at the foot of the Canaparia, two tofts nigh to the Perfect Pillar;[2] also the Parish of the lower Camellaria, and the property of the same Camellaria, so that no injury be done to the dwellers in the same Camellaria by the dwellers in the upper Camellaria;[3] also the garden of Saint Laurence or above Saint Laurence; the land which was

[9] *Mirabilia*, p. 96.
[440] *Cum casis.*
[1] *Cum casalinis. Casalinum, locus ubi casae aedificatae fuerunt.* Ducange, *Glossarium.*
[2] *Juxta columnam perfectissimam.* Possibly the Phocas Column.
[3] *Mirabilia*, p. 90. See also note 425.

formerly an olive-yard from the cavern as far as
Saint Saviour; the land above the olive-yard as
far as the bath or basin; the garden of Saint
Sergius or behind Saint Sergius, and the garden
among the columns,[4] as far as the Apse [5] and as
far as the Mamertine Prison, upon the which a
question was long moved between you and the
church of Saint Mary of the Capitol, and was set
at rest by an amicable composition by the dele-
gation of Pope Celestine, of happy memory, our
predecessor, through our beloved sons J. by the
title of Saint Stephen *in Celiomonte*, and S. by
the title of Saint Praxed, Cardinal Priests, as in
the writing of the said Cardinals, thereof made,
is more fully contained; to you and through you
to your church, by authority apostolic, we do
confirm.

3. *Table of Relics at the Basilica of the Lateran.*[6]

THIS Basilica of our Saviour and Lord Jesus
Christ, and of Saint John Baptist, and of
the blessed John the Evangelist, is ennobled by

[4] Probably remains of the Porticus of Concord.

[5] Jordan suggests the apse of the *Secretarium Senatus*, possibly the same as a *porticus curva* mentioned in Cassiodorus. *Topographie*, ii. 457, 481.

[6] The following table, inscribed in mosaic with gold letters upon a blue ground, was formerly in a

these most holy and venerable sanctuaries: in the
first place this Wooden Altar, which God's holy
pontiffs and martyrs had from the time of the
Apostles, and whereon through the crypts and
divers hiding-places they celebrated masses when
the rage of persecution was threatening them;
upon the which, above, is the Table of our Lord,
whereat Christ supped with his disciples in the
day of [his passion]. And in this[7] altar are two

portico behind the high altar in the ancient apse of
the Lateran Basilica. It is now placed in the new
cloister to the left of the door of the Sacristy. A
second similar table on the right hand records in
verse the rebuilding of the church by Nicholas IV.
in 1291. The two tables are apparently contemporary, though the letters are in some cases a little
different in form. The Latin original has been
printed in Rosponi, *De Basilica Lateran.* 48; Crescembeni, *S. Giovanni a Porta Latina*, 135; Forcella,
Iscrizioni delle Chiese, viii, 14. But the copy which
follows this Translation is believed to be more correct. As to the Lateran relics, see pp. 65, 131, 155.

[7] *Cena[vit cum discipulis in die ca3na3 in hoc]
autem.* The word *ca3na3* has been misread *caenae*
in the printed copies. The *in* which follows is
superfluous. The sign 3 might stand for any omitted
letters, as, for example, such a word as *catenarum*.
Perhaps the word was originally *carnis*; for the line
which begins with *vit* and ends with *hoc* appears
to be a restoration, containing forms of letters
found in the other table, but not elsewhere in this.

phials of the blood and water from Chrift's fide.
Moreover there is part of Chrift's Cradle, the
Coat without Seam, and his purple robe. Moreover there is the napkin that was about his head,
and the towel that he wafhed his difciples' feet
withal. Moreover there is of the five barley
loaves; and of the afhes and blood of Saint John
Baptift; and his Raiment of Camel's hair; of
manna from the tomb of Saint John the Evangelift, and his Coat, and alfo part of the Chain
wherewith he came bound from Ephefus, and the
fhears[8] that he was fhorn withal by commandment of Cæfar Domitian. And beneath this
altar is the Ark of the Covenant,[9] wherein are the
Two Tables of the Teftament, Mofes' Rod,
and the Rod of Aaron. There is alfo the Golden
Candleftick, and the Golden Cenfer full of incenfe,
and an urn of gold full of Manna, and some of
the Shewbread. Now this ark, with the candleftick and the things aforefaid, together with the
four prefent Pillars,[150] did Titus and Vefpafian

[8] *Forcipes. Mirabilia*, p. 66.

[9] *Mirabilia*, p. 65.

[150] *Mirabilia*, p. 66, note 119. Thefe bronze
columns, which are plain fluted, were formerly at
the great arch of the nave near the high altar, and
were placed by Clement VIII. at the altar of the
Sacrament. (Rofponi, *De Bafilica Lateran*, 45.)
Benjamin of Tudela believed them to be from

make to be brought of the Jews from Jerusalem to the City, even as it is seen to this day in the Triumphal Arch that is nigh unto the church of Saint Mary New, for their victory and for a perpetual remembrance of them, set up by the Roman Senate and People.

(*The original Latin inscription is printed on the next page.*)

Solomon's temple. (See p. 115.) They have now composite capitals in which a star (the badge of Clement VIII.) is introduced.

Literal Copy of the Original Table of Relics at the Lateran Baſilica.

HEC BASILICA SALVATORIS DNĪ NRĪ IESV XPĪ
SCĪQ; IOHĪS BAPTISTE ATQ; BEATI IOHAN
NIS EVANGELISTE HIS SACRO SANCTIS
AC VENERABILIBVS SANCTVARIIS INSIGNI
TA CONSISTIT IN PRIMIS HOC ALTARE LIGNEO
QUOD SANCTI DEI PONTIFICES ꞇ MARTYRES AB APO
STOLOR; TEMPORE HABVERVNT IN QVO P̄ CRIP
TAS ꞇ DIVERSA LATIBVLA MISSAS CELEBRA
BANT P̄SECUTIONIS RABIE IMMANENTE SVP QVO
DE SVP̄ER EST MENSA DOMINI IN QVA XP̄S CENA
VIT CUM DISCIPVLIS IN DIE CA;NA; IN HOC
AVTEM IN ALTARI SVNT DE SANGVINE ꞇ AQVA
DE LATERE XPĪ AMPULLE DUE ITEM EST IBI DE
CVNA XPĪ TVNICA INCONSVTILIS ET PVRPVRE
VM VESTIMENTVM EIVS ITEM EST IBI SVDARI
VM QVOD FVIT SVPER CAPVT EIVS ꞇ LINTEVM
VNDE PEDES DISCIPVLOR; LAVIT ITEM EX QVINQVE
PANIBVS ORDEACIIS ITEM DE CINERIBVS ꞇ SANGVI
NE SANCTI IOHANNIS BAPTISTE ꞇ CILICIVM EIVS DE PI
LIS CAMELORU DE MAÑA SEPULCHRI SCĪ IOHĪS EVĀ
GELISTE ET TVNICA EIVS ꞇ ETIAM PARS CATENE CVM
QUA LEGATVS VENIT AB EFESO FORCIPES CV̄ QVIBVS
TONSVS FVIT DE MANDATO CESARIS DOMITIANI SVB ISTO
NEMPE ALTARI EST ARCA FEDERIS IN QVA SVNT
DVE TABVLE TESTAMENTI VIRGA MOYSI ꞇ VIRGA AA
RON EST IBI CANDELABRV̄ AVREŪ ꞇ THVRIBVLV̄
AUREV̄ THYMEAMATE PLENV̄ ꞇ URNA AVREA PLE
NA MANNA ꞇ DE PANIBVS PROPOSITIONV̄ HANC
AUTEM ARCĀ CV̄ CANDELABRO ET HIIS QUE DICTA
SV̄T CŪ QUATVOR PRESENTIBVS COLV̄PNIS TI
TVS ꞇ VESPASIANVS A IVDEIS ASPORTARI FE
CERVNT DE HĒRVSOLIMA AD VRBĒ SICVT VS
QVE HODIE CERNITVR IN TRIVMPHALI FORNI
CE QUI EST IVXTA ECCLESIAM SANCTE MA
RIE NOVE OB VICTORIAM ET PERPETVVM
MONVMENTVM EORVM A SENATV POPVLOQVE
ROMANO POSITVM

V. Medieval Plan of Rome.

THE map of Rome at the end of this volume is copied (with partial reduction in height but not in width) from one of thofe edited by De Roffi in his valuable feries of medieval plans of Rome. (*Piante di Roma*, tav. ii. 1.) De Roffi's drawing is itfelf a reduction (two-thirds of the original) of a plan contained in a manufcript of the Cofmography of Ptolemy, preferved in the National Library at Paris (No. 4802), which has the arms of Henry II. of France upon the binding.

In the fixteenth chapter of the Treatife publifhed with the Plans, the learned editor gives an interefting account of thofe manufcripts and printed editions of the Latin Tranflation of Ptolemy's work illuftrated with maps, which were multiplied in the laft thirty years of the fifteenth century. Of the prefent plan of Rome copies exift in other manufcripts, one of which, from the Urbinate MS. No. 277, in the Vatican Library is alfo given in De Roffi's work. This book has the date 1472, and was painted in the study of Hugo Comminellus de Maceriis, to whom De Rossi also attributes the Paris manuscript. A slight variation in the map of Rome furnishes evidence of the later date of the Paris copy. The Ponte Sisto, which was founded in 1473 and opened in 1475, is absent in the Urbino manuscript, but appears in that of Paris, which must therefore have been drawn somewhat after the other. But the original design, from which both are taken, is thought by De Rossi to have been made between 1455 and 1464.

The period to which our plan belongs is therefore precisely that which witnessed the commencement of the more critical studies of classical literature and epigraphy by which the authority of the *Mirabilia* was overthrown. But the plans bear no impress of the new learning; and the names which are ascribed to the monuments belong, as De Rossi has observed, to " the terminology which may be called Mirabilian." They were evidently prepared by a draughtsman and intended for readers who were still guided in their Roman archæology by the old Hand-book. For this reason they form a suitable illustration to the present volume.

The Paris plan has been chosen, as being more carefully drawn than that of Urbino. Like most of the medieval plans of Rome, it is in the nature of a bird's-eye view, taken from the side of the Porta del Popolo. Very little attempt is made to represent the actual shape of the city as shown by the circuit of walls; and in filling in this area, the system adopted has been to select the objects which were thought most important, the ordinary houses and the minor churches being altogether omitted, and no indication being given of the streets, with one exception, that the route from the Ponte di S. Angelo towards the Capitol, through the Campo di Fiori, and the Jews' Piazza (Piazza del Pianto) is indicated by a line and two squares. Three Palaces only, the Lateran, the Vatican, and the Senators' Palace at the Capitol, are shown, with the principal basilicas and most famous monuments of antiquity. The hills are indicated by a dark shading. The monuments are represented, not by a mere note of their situation or area, but by slight sketches of their general form and appearance, which are often of much value, as showing the condition of the buildings in the middle of the fifteenth century.

The views of the Capitol and of the Forum are especially interesting. In the former the restored palace of the Senators, flanked by its two western towers, has on the left the church of St. Mary in Ara celi, with its long flight of marble steps, and on the right a ruin consisting of some columns and an architrave, which can scarcely be other than the last remains of the Capitoline Temple.[151] Beyond is seen the Forum. The churches immediately behind the Capitol are omitted. On the right, between the Capitol and the Palatine, is a building which the draughtsman has represented as an arch, perhaps intending it for that of Severus, but which, from its situation, may have been meant, in the original design, for another monument, possibly the remains of the temple of Castor, or of the Basilica Julia, the Cannapara of the *Mirabilia*. On the left, the mass formed by the temple of Faustina, with the round church of SS. Cosmas and Damian, and the basilica of Constantine, is very faithfully shown. Opposite Faustina, in the middle of the Campo Vaccino, is a tower, probably a residue of the fortress of the Frangipani;[2] and beyond, drawn on a small scale as a distant part of the same sketch, are the church of S. Maria Nuova, and the Arch of Titus, with the buildings which united them; while to the right rises the Palatine hill, occupied by the " Greater Palace " of the *Mirabilia*. In the next line, beyond the Forum group, towers the Colosseum, with a magnitude proportioned to its celebrity and importance.

[151] *Mirabilia*, p. 88, note 171 and p. 178.

[2] See p. 99.

The mass of buildings at the Lateran, and the nearer and more detailed group of the Vatican and the Borgo, are no less inftructive. In the latter the ancient pyramid, called the Sepulchre of Romulus, is feen near the caftle of Saint Angelo.

Between the Porta del Popolo and the Porta Pia, may be ftudied a group of ruins which furnifh a fuggeftion of what then remained of the Salluftian Palace and of the *Domus Pinciana*. Outfide the walls the principal churches and other places of intereft to pilgrims are fhown; but the moft characteriftic object confifts of a length of broken aqueduct, at the fide of which is a heap of earth under which is believed to be a temple, a typical and truly Mirabilian picture of the Roman Campagna.

In the original map the names of many, but not all, of the objects delineated are written againft them in Latin, in a hand by no means eafy to read. In the following table the plan is divided into fixteen parts, of which the firft four are thofe along the top; and the objects in each part, the higher objects being taken firft, are indicated by the Latin names ufed in the original map, or by a modern defcription, or by both. The names in brackets [ ] are fupplied from the companion map in the Urbinate Manufcript mentioned above.

A. 1. An aqueduct and a heap of ruins, inscribed *Sub hoc cumulo est templum*. *Porta maior*.

A. 2. *Coloffeum parvum, Sancta Crux in Ierufalem* (the Amphitheatrum Caftrenfe, and Church of Holy Crofs in Jerufalem). *P. Sancti Johannis Laterani* (the Gate and Palace of Saint John Lateran). [*Sancta Sanctorum, fcala hæc per quam Chriftus ad Pilatum*], the chapel of Saint Laurence, called Holy of Holies (with a dome over it), and the Scala Sancta. The "Horfe of Conftantine."[4] The Arch of Dolabella with a tower over it.[5]

A. 3. *Theatrum* [*theatrum gladiatorum, theatro dove battagle mortali faceano*], the circus of Maxentius. *S. Sebaftianus. S. Annunciata*. [*Domine quo vadis*].

Porta latina. *Porta Dazza* [*Porta Appia*]. *Porta S. Pauli*. *Palatium Augufti (?) Thermæ Antonianæ* (Antoninianæ). The Aventine Hill, *S. Saus* (S. Sabba, in old Italian, Santo Save), [*Arcus Tarquinii Prifci, S. Alefii*].

A. 4. Outfide the walls, a pillar on the way to Saint Paul, [*apud hanc crucem S. Paulus prouta*[6]

---

[4] This object is added from the drawing in the Urbino Manufcript.

[5] Perhaps in the original drawing S. Stefano Rotondo may have been reprefented here.

[6] De Rofii fuggefts the words *prout ante mortem dixerat*, and the emendation *velum* for *telum* (*Piante*,

defunctus telum mulieri reddidit]. Ponte della Moletta, with a building near the bridge. *S. Paulus*. Further off, the Tre Fontane, [*fontes ubi decoliatus eft S. Paulus*], *S. Naftafius, Scala cœli*.

Within the walls, *Remi fepulcrum. Teftaccius mons*.

B. 1. *Porta S. Laurentii. Aquæ duɛtus*.

B. 2. *Coloffeum. Trophea cymbrica* [*Arcus cymbrius*]. *S. Petrus in vincula. Turris comitum. S. Adrianus* (S. Lorenzo in Miranda). SS. Cofma and Damiano. *Templum Pacis* (Bafilica of Conftantine). S. Maria Nuova. *Ara Celi*.

B. 3. *Trax Arcus* [*Arcus Thracius*] (Arch of Conftantine, commonly called Arco de trafi). Arch of Titus. *Palatium maior* (Palatine Hill and Imperial palaces). [*Spelunca Cacci*] under the Aventine. *Templum Sybillarum* [*Sybillæ*], S. Maria in Cofmedin. [*Pons Sanctæ Mariæ*]. *Hic se iecit horatius in amnem*.

Tower of the Frangipani. Arch of Severus, or Bafilica Julia. *S. Georgius* [*Templum Severi-*

p 146). See before p. 144. The little building between the pillar and St. Paul may have been the church of S. Menna, reftored by Leo III. (*Lib. Pontif.*), and named in the Einfiedeln Itinerary. Urlichs, *Codex*, 68; Jordan, *Topographie*, ii. 258; Martinelli, *Roma Sacra*, 377.

anum]. Double arch in the Velabrum [*Templum Iovis quod et domus faveliorum*].⁷ [*Pons Iudeorum*]. *S. bartolomeus.* [*Pons tranſtiberim*].

B. 4. *Porta Portuenſis. Porta S. Pancratii.* The Church of St. Pancras. [*S. Ceciliæ, S. Franciſci*]. *S. Griſogonus. S. Petrus in montorio ubi cruci afixus eſt.*

S. Maria tranſtiberim ubi in natali Chriſti oleum manavit [*unde oleum fluxit in tiberim in nocte nativitatis domini*].

C. 1. Outſide the walls, *S. Laurentius. Porta Numentana* (Porta Pia). *Thermæ Diocletianæ.*

C. 2. On the hill, S. Maria Maggiore. The Marble Horſes. [*Menſa Neronis*]. *Militiæ turris* [*Militiæ palatium*].

In the valley, *Palatium Cæſaris* (Forum of Auguſtus). *Columna Antoniana*⁸ (Column of Trajan). *S. Marcus.*

*Minerva. Bruti ſepulchrum.*⁹ *S. Apoſtolus.*

---

⁷ The two objects which in one map stand for the church of S. Giorgio in Velabro, and the arch near it, are identified in the other as the Portico of Octavia then called the temple of Severus, and the Theatre of Marcellus, in which the Savelli were already eſtabliſhed.

⁸ *Antoniniana.* The names of the two great columns ſeem to be accidentally tranſpoſed.

⁹ See note 164.

Traiana Columna (Column of Marcus Aurelius). *Palatium Adriani* (Arch of Claudius?).[460] *S. Maria Rotonda.*

C. 3. *S. Angelus ubi forum piscatorum* (Portico of Octavia). The Ponte Sisto. *Porta Septignana.*

S. Euſtachius. Area iudea. (Piazza del Pianto). *S. Iacopus de Septignana.*

S. Lorenzo in Damaſo. Platea, i.e. campus de flore.

C. 4. *Ianiculus mons. Porta Sancti Spiritus.* [*Lacus neronis*]. *Palatium neronis* [*Agulia. S. Petri*].

D. 1. *S. Agneſa. Porta Salaria, Porta Pinciana.* [*Pincis*] (The ruins of the Palaces on the Pincian Hill).

D. 2. *S. Silveſter ubi caput eſt batiſtæ Iohanis.* Arch in the Via Flaminia.[1] *S. Laurentius in lucina. S. Apollinaris ubi manſit maomecus.*[2] [*Sancti Auguſtini. S. Trifonis*].

[*Sanctæ Mariæ Populi*]. *Porta Flamminia* [*quæ et Porta populi*]. *Turris ſpiritus neronis* [*Turris ubi umbra neronis diu manſitavit*].[3]

[460] See p. 12, note 23.

[1] See p. 11, note 22.

[2] I have not found anything to explain this deſcription.

[3] The ſtory of Nero haunting the neighbourhood of the Porta del Popolo is not told in the *Mirabilia.*

D. 3. *Agon. S. Agnefa.* [*Domus Orfina*] Monte Giordano.⁴ *Tiber fluvius. S. Celfus* [*Sancti iohannis. S. blafii*]. Bridge of S. Angelo. *Caftellum S. Angeli. Porta Caftelli* [*Porta collina quæ et caftelli*].⁵ *Sepulcrum Romuli.*

D. 4. [*Hofpital fancti fpiritus*]. *Porta viridaria* [*quæ et Sancti Petri*]. [*Nova turris. Palatium pontificis*].

Outſide the wall, *Theatrum,* Hadrian's Circus.

Frontifpiece.

The bronze doors of St. Peter's, made for Eugenius IV. in 1447, have among other ornaments a baſ-relief of the Paſſion of St. Peter by Antonio Filarete. In this work, to mark the locality, the foreground is occupied by a row of objects conceived in the ſpirit of the *Mirabilia.* Theſe are the 'Sepulchre of Remus' with a figure of Roma before it, the Tiber with ſhields and arms floating on it, the 'Temple of Hadrian', the Terebinth, and the 'Sepulchre of Romulus'. The laſt three objects ſymbolize the place of Saint Peter's crucifixion.⁶

⁴ This object, repreſented as a ſquare caſtle, is added from the plan of the Urbino manuſcript.

⁵ The Porta Collina of the *Mirabilia* and *Ordo Romanus* is not this gate, but that cloſing the bridge on the ſide of the Borgo. See pp. 8, 168.

⁶ See pp. 7, 75-79, and note 144.

ABOUT 1475

THE CITY OF ROME FROM A PLAN USED ABOUT 1474

INDEX.

INDEX.

Abdon and Sennen, 50-55.
Abſolom, ſtatue of, 156.
Aerarium, 95.
Aeſculapius, temple of, 100, 116.
Albiſton, 32, 102, 103.
Alexandrine circus, 23, 169.
Alexandrine Thermae, 18, 82.
All Saints' Day, its origin, 49, 50.
Anaſtaſius IV. his tomb, 79.
Antonine column, 21, 25, 84.
Aqua Salvia, 30, 134.
Ara Celi, 38, 90, 141.
Arca Noe, 2, 161n.
Arch of Antoninus, 12.
 Aurea, 161, 167.
 Claudius, 12n, 195.
 Camillus, 21.
 Conſtantine, 11, 171, 193.
 Dripping, 30, 32.
 Druſus, 10, 30n.
 Hand of Fleſh, 12, 170.
 Gallienus, 163
 Gold Bread, 13.
 Latona (*in Lathone*), 100, 175.
 Marcus Aurelius, 11n.
 Nerva, 161, 170.
 Pity or Piety, 14, 84, 168.
 the Seven Lamps, 11, 100, 171.
 Severus, 11n, 170, 180.
 Severus in Velabro, 13n.
 Theodoſius and Gratian, 10, 159, 169.
 Titus, 11, 100, 105, 171.
 Titus at the circus, 10.

Arch, Roman, 32, 69.
Arches, triumphal, 9-15.
Arco dei l'antani, 93, 110, 163n.
Argentaria inſula, 92.
Argentarii clivus, 91, 170, 177.
Auguratorium, 102.
S. Auguſtine cited, 37.
Auguſtum, mauſoleum of Auguſtus, 80.
Auguſtus, viſion of, 35.
Aurelia Oreſtilla, her houſe, 111.
Aventine hill, 110.

Balneanapolis, 17.
S. Baſil, convent of, 92, 162n, 167.
Bede, his tomb, 125.
Breeches Towers, 11.
Bridges of Rome, 24, 25.
Brutus' ſepulchre, 85n, 194.
Buſhels, ruins ſo called, 108.

Caccabariorum regio, 113.
Caelian hill, 106.
Caeſar, Forum of, 99.
Caeſar, *see* Julius.
Calcarare, 85.
Camellaria, 90, 177.
 Upper and Lower, 177n, 181.
Camillanum, 21, 85.
Campus Martius, 84, 168.

Cannapara, 31*n*, 32, 89, 96, 178, 181.
Cantarus at the Vatican, 73, 173.
Capitol, 16, 86-90.
Capitoline hill granted to abbey of St. Mary, 176-179.
Capitoline temple, ruins of, 88, 178, 190.
Carcer Tullianus, 112.
Cartulary tower, 11, 101.
Catacombs, 26-29.
Caterino, S. Maria in, 114.
Catiline, palace of, 97.
Cemeteries or catacombs, 26-29.
Centum Gradus, 179.
Chromatius, palace of, 114, 159, 169.
Churches:
  S. Abbacyrus, 167.
  S. Agnes in Agone, 137.
  S. Agnes without the Walls, 149
  S. Anastasius, 134.
  S. Angelo in Pescheria, 113, 145.
  S. Balbina, 149.
  S. Bartholomew, 116, 145.
  S. Benedict in Piscinula, 116.
  S. Catherine dei Funari, 86.
  S. Cesarius, 102.
  S. Cosmas, 100.
  S. Cross in Jerusalem, 20, 145
  S. Gregory, 129, 143.
    in Martio, 165, 174.
  S. John at Janiculum, 2, 22.
    Lateran, see Lateran Basilica.
    at Latin Gate, 7, 142.
  S. Laurence in Fonte, 151.
    in Laterano (Sancta Sanctorum), 131, 132, 174.
    in Lucina, 151.
    in Miranda, 106.
    in Panisperna, 147.
    in Porticu (in Piscibus), 172.

Churches (continued):
  S. Laurence without the Walls, 151.
  S. Lucia in Orphea, 162*n*.
  S. Mark, 85, 147.
  S. Mary in Campo, 92.
    in Capitolio, (in ara celi), 38, 90, 141.
    of Egypt, 111*n*.
    in Fontana, 108.
    de Gradellis, 111.
    Imperatrice, 165*n*.
    de Inferno, 97, 145.
    Major, 107, 121, 134.
    Sopra Minerva, 85.
    New, 100, 135.
    in schola Graeca, 111, 112*n*.
    in Trastevere, 115, 148.
    Transpontina, 77, 137.
    Virgariorum, 173.
  S. Menna, 193*n*.
  S. Nicolas in calcaria, 86.
    in carcere, 112, 158*n*.
  Pantheon, 46, 74, 82, 135.
  S. Paul, 68, 133.
  S. Pellegrino, 75.
  S. Peter in the Vatican, 67, 73, 125.
    ad vincula, 108, 137, 152.
  S. Praxedes, 138.
  S. Pudentiana, 138.
  S. Quiricus, 93.
  S. Saviour in porticu, 97.
    de statera, 97, 181, 182.
  S. Sebastian at the Catacombs, 151.
    on the Palatine, 101.
  SS. Sergius and Bacchus, 95, 179.
  S. Silvester in capite, 137.
  S. Sixtus, 141.
  S. Spirito, 148.
  S. Stephen alle Carrozze, 112*n*.
    in piscinulis, 114.
    Round, 16, 111
  S. Valentine, 8.
  S. Vitus in macello, 145.

Cicero, temple of, 112, 158.
Cimbrum, 107, 163.
Cincius or Cinthius, prefect, 79.
Circi and *stadia*, 23.
Circus Antonini, 114.
Circus Maximus, 103, 105.
Cleopatra, 57, 58.
Collina porta, 8, 168, 196.
Colosseum, 62-64, 171.
Colossus, 63, 64n, 102.
Concord, temple of, 92, 95, 170.
Constantine, basilica of, 20, 100.
    conversion of, 68, 122.
    Thermae of, 21, 109.
Consuls of the Romans, 85.
Cornuti, baths of, 34.
Craticula, temple of, 113, 158.
Crescentius, castle of, 24, 76.
Curtius, legend of, 97, 98.

Deacons, eighteen Cardinal, 160.
Diocletian, baths of, 108, 138.
Domine quo vadis, 7, 27, 143.

Elephantus Herbarius, 88n, 112, 178.
England, Dominican monasteries in, 142.
Esquiline hill (Monte Superaggio), 17, 147.

Fabii, temple of, 95.
Fatal temple, 11, 94, 170.
Faunus, temple of, 108, 112, 113.
Faustina, temple of, 100.
Flaminian circus, 23, 24, 34, 86, 113, 158.
Fors Fortuna, temple of, 116.

Forum of Augustus, 92n, 161n.
    of Caesar, 99, 170.
    of Nerva, 93.
    of Trajan, 21, 91, 93, 161, 167, 170.
Forum Romanum, 96n.
Frontespizio di Nerone, 109.
Frangipane, tower of, 99.
Fullonia at the Lateran, 79, 163.

Gates of Rome, 6-9.
Gorgon, temple of, 115.
Gradellae, place so called, 111, 158n.

Hadrian, temple of, 91.
Hell, place so called, 97, 145.
Hescodius or Estodius, a medieval historian, 2.
Holovitreum, 114, 159.
Holy places in Rome, 29-34.

Innocent II., his tomb, 79.
Insula Milicena, 159.

Janus Quadrifrons, 13n, 111.
Janus, temple of, 90, 99, 171.
Jews, their ancient league with Rome, 93.
    their place for saluting the Pope, 169.
Jews' Bridge, 24, 113.
    Piazza, 189, 195.
    Quarter, 24.
Judas Maccabeus, 93.
Julian, beguiled by Faunus, 108.
Julius Caesar, inthroned pontiff, 89.
    killed in the Capitol, 90.
    his memorial (obelisk), 71, 73.

Last Supper, Easter ceremony, 163-165.
Lateran Basilica, its foundation, 65 bronze pillars, 66, 155.
relics, 65, 66, 106, 131-133, 182-186.
Lateranus Campus, 165, 174.
Laurence, place of his martyrdom, 18n, 33, 110, 147.
Legend of SS. Abdon and Sennen, 50-55.
S. Agnes and her priest, 150.
Augustus and the sibyl, 25, 90.
the Bull Gate, 7.
the Bells of the Capitol (*Salvatio Romae*), 46, 54.
King Charles and the ring, 128.
Constantine and S. Silvester, 32, 68, 122.
Curtius, 97, 98.
S. Dominic, 142.
the foundation of S. Mary Major, 121, 122, 132, 133
the foundation of Rome, 1-5.
the foundation of the Pantheon, 46.
the fountain of oil in Trastevere, 34, 115.
S. Gregory, 15, 129, 143, 149.
S. Helen, 124.
the horse called Constantine's, 42.
the horses of marble, 39, 40.
S. John at the Latin Gate, 7, 66, 143, 184.
Julian the Apostate, 108.
S. Laurence, 18, 33, 34, 56, 147, 151.
S. Lucy and the Hand of Flesh, 12, 13.
Legend of the Mausoleum of Augustus, 81, 155.
Nero and the Frog, 19, 20.
S. Paul and the kerchief, 144, 192.
the dedication of S. Peter *ad vincula*, 57-62.
S. Peter's chains, 60.
S. Peter's corn-heap, 76n.
Phidias and Praxiteles, 39.
Philip, emperor and martyr, 51.
the taking of Jerusalem, 154.
Pope Joan, 139.
the image of Romulus, 21, 136.
S. Sebastian, 31, 114, 151.
S. Silvester and the dragon, 98, 144.
Simon Magus, 135, 136, 171.
S. Sixtus, 29, 50.
S. Stephen, pope, 151, 152.
the Three Fountains, 30, 134.
Trajan's pity and justice, 14.
Virgil's witchcraft, 17.
Lentulus, palace of, 111.
Leo Prothus, Descent of, 177.
Leonine city, or Peter's Porch, 6, 9.
Livy referred to, 4, 5.
Lycaonia Insula, 116.

Macellum Livianum, 163.
Magnanapoli, 17n.
Mahomet, his abode, 195.

Majorent, an oracle of Apollo, 83.
Mamertinus, prison of, 33, 170, 182.
Maps of Rome in the middle age, 187.
Marius, trophies of, 107, 163.
Market place of Capitol, 88, 89, 177.
Mausoleum of Augustus, 80, 81.
  Hadrian, 78.
Mensa Imperatoris (Neronis), 109, 194.
Merulana, 163.
Meta, pyramid so called, 75, 76.
Meta Sudans, 171.
Mica Aurea, 3, 22.
Minerva Chacidica, temple of, 85.
Moneta, temple of, 88.
Monte Cavallo, 109.
Montorio, 22n.

Naumachia, region of, 75.
Nero, his camp, 148.
  his Chancery, 84.
  his Ghost, 195.
  his Obelisk, 77, 159, 168.
  his Wardrobe, 71.
Nerva, arch of, 161, 167, 170.
  Forum of, 93.
  tomb of, 81.
Nimrod or Nembroth, a founder of Rome, 3.
Noah, a founder of Rome, 1.
Noah's Ark, ruin so called, 2, 161n.

Obelisk of the Piazza del Panteon, 85n.
  of the Vatican, 71.
Obelisks of the Circus Maximus, 104, 105.
Olympia, baths of, 33, 109.

Ordo Romanus, extracts from, 157-175.
Orphanotrophium, 106.
Orphei domus (lacus), 162, 175.
Orrigo, tower of, 111.
Ovid cited or alluded to, 9, 80, 88, 89, 90, 99, 113, 116.

Palaces of Rome, 19-22.
Palatina, 169.
Palatium majus (casa major), 19, 102.
Palatine hill, 101, 102.
Pallas, temple of (Regia), 98, 99n, 101.
Pantheon, 48, 74, 82, 135.
  its foundation and history, 47-50.
Parione, 169.
S. Paul, basilica of, 68, 133.
  martyrdom of, 134, 144.
  his cloak left at Troas, 134.
  his kerchief, 144, 192.
Peace, temple of, 100, 136, 193.
Pergula aurea, 112.
S. Peter, basilica of, 67, 125.
  body of, 67, 126.
  Cantharus of, 73.
  his place of martyrdom, 77, 137, 194.
S. Peter's chains, 60.
  cornheap, 76n.
  Parvise or Paradise, 73.
  Porch, 6, 9.
Philip, first Christian emperor, 51.
Phocas column, 181n.
Pierleone's house, 112, 113n, 158n.
Pilate's house, 147.
Pinciana domus, 8n, 191.
Pincius, king, his palace, 8.

Pinea or Pigna, 82, 169.
Pifcina in Traftevere, 116.
Ponte Sifto, 24.
Porticus apfidata, 161.
    Crinorum, 88.
    Gallatorum, 157, 158.
    S. Petri (major), 159, 173.
    Octaviae, 112, 113, 158.
Prifon, Mamertine, 33, 170, 182.
Proceffions, Papal, 157-175.

Ravennatium templum (urbs), 34, 115.
Regia, 99*n*.
Relics, table of at the Lateran, 182-186.
Remus, fepulchre (or temple) of, 7.
Riparmea, or *Ripa Romea*, 25.
Romulus, palace (or temple) of, 20, 100.
    fepulchre of, 7, 75, 168.
    ftory of his image, 21-136.
Rofe, the lady, her monaftery, 86.
Roftra, 85.

Sancta Sanctorum at Lateran, 131, 174, 192.
    holy image in, 132, 174.
Saturn, temple of, 92, 95.
Saffia, diftrict fo called, 24.
Scala Sancta, 192.
Schola Graeca, 111.
S. Sebaftian, 114.
Sedes ftercoraria, 129.
Senators' palace, 16.
Septizonium, 31, 56, 84, 102.
Sefforian palace, 20, 106.

SS. Sergius and Bacchus, property of their church, 180, 182.
Sergius, garden of, 179, 182.
Severus' arch, its medieval condition, 95, 170*n*, 180.
Sibyl, temple of, 112, 158, 193.
Silex, by S. Lucia in Orphea, 162.
    by the bafilica of Conftantine 171.
Solomon's pillars at the Lateran, 155.
Stadia and *circi*, 23.
Statera, 96, 181, 182.
Statue of Abfolom, 156.
    Conftantine, 42, 156.
    Hygieia (Giuftiniani Palace), 41*n*.
    Marble horfes, 39, 109.
    Marforio, 94, 137.
    Saturn and Bacchus (River Gods), 109.
    Samfon, 154.
    Woman with Serpents, 39, 41.
Statues of Ancient Rome, 26, 87, 88.
Suetonius referred to, 36, 38.
Sun, temple of, 102.
Superagius mons (Efquiline), 17, 107.

Taberna Meritoria, 115.
Tabularium, 16*n*; and fee *Camellaria*.
Tellus, houfe or temple of, 31*n*, 33, 96.
Templum Majus, 178.
Terebinth, 76.
Theatre of Balbus, 114*n*, 159*n*.
    Marcellus, 23*n*, 34*n*, 113*n*, 158*n*.
    Pompey, 83.
Theatres, 23, 24.

Thermae, 17-18, 106.
Titus, his palace at the Catacombs, 22, 154.
Tofula or *Tofella*, 92.
Tofetti family, their tower, 12.
Tower, Cartulary, 11, 101.
    of the Field, 169n.
    Cencio Frangipane, 99.
    Orrigo, 111.
    the Tofetti, 12.
Towers of the Breeches, 11.
Trajan, column of, 21, 25, 91.
    forum of, 21, 91, 93, 110, 161.
    legend of, 14.
Tre fontane, 30, 134.
Traftevere, 115, 116.
Trevi or *Trivium*, 108.
Tudela, Benjamin of, 153-156.

Varro cited or referred to, 3, 4.
Vatican Bafilica, 67, 70, 125.

Velum Aureum (Velabrum), 30, 113.
Venus, Garden of, 109.
Venus and Rome, temple of, 20, 100.
Vefpafian, his palace at the catacombs, 22, 154.
    his tomb, 148.
Vefta, temple of, 98.
Via Majer, 166n.
    Quirinalis, 167.
    Salara, vetus et nova, 8.
    Sancta, 166n, 171.
    Sacra, 172.
Vicus Canarius, 30.
    Latericius, 33.
    Patricius, 33.
Virgil, a wizard, 17.
Virgil alluded to, 4, 101.
Viridarium of the Vatican, 8.
Volufian, 20n, 148.

Walls of Rome, 5, 6.

Westminster: Printed by Nichols and Sons, 25, Parliament Street.

www.ingramcontent.com/pod-product-compliance
Lightning Source LLC
Chambersburg PA
CBHW031738230426
43669CB00007B/388